THE
NEW
LAO
TZU

THE NEW LAO TZU

A CONTEMPORARY TAO TE CHING

RAY GRIGG

CHARLES E. TUTTLE CO., INC.
BOSTON · RUTLAND, VERMONT · TOKYO, JAPAN

First published in 1995 by Charles E. Tuttle Co., Inc. of
Rutland, Vermont and Tokyo, Japan, with editorial offices
at 153 Milk Street, Boston, Massachusetts 02109

Library of Congress Cataloging-in-Publication Data

Grigg, Ray, 1938–
   The new Lao Tzu : a contemporary Tao te ching / Ray
   Grigg.
   p. cm.
   Includes bibliographical references and indexes.
   ISBN 0–8048–3034–7
   1. Lao-tzu. Tao te ching. I. Title.
BL1900.L35G75 1995
299'.51482 – DC20   94–46615
                                        CIP

00 99 98 97 96 95 1 3 5 7 9 10 8 6 4 2

All ink paintings are © 1995 Bill Gaetz and are reproduced
by kind permission of the artist.

Design by Jill Winitzer
Printed in the United States

CONTENTS

INTRODUCTION

About 2,500 years ago, according to legend, Lao Tzu left his native China for India, dismayed with the unsettling changes that were taking place in his country. At its last outpost he hurriedly wrote a summary of his wisdom, left it with the lone gatekeeper, and disappeared forever into the wilderness.

If this scenario were repeated today in the West, what would Lao Tzu leave behind as the written record of his wisdom so modern readers could be instructed by his insights? The answer to this question has guided the writing of *The New Lao Tzu*.

A contemporary version of the old classic would read in substance and spirit like a translation of the original, but in style and detail it would feel modern, perhaps with a slight Chinese accent. The archaic images and metaphors of an historic China would be replaced by ones familiar to the West. Social and political commentaries would reflect present realities.

The resonant density of the sage's phrasing would still be present, however, the poetry would be more fluid and explicit. The logic of Lao Tzu's arguments would be more linear, and easier to follow, but the teachings would retain their unique measure of profound simplicity. So, in brief, *The New Lao Tzu* reads more like a loose interpretation than a strict translation.

Purists may respond with indignation at such treatment of the *Lao Tzu*. However, scholarly justification already exists for taking liberties with the sage's words. The usual attempts at translating the traditional texts by adhering to the actual order and logic of its Chinese characters have been profoundly unsatisfactory. Indeed, such attempts have made the *Lao Tzu* almost unreadable. Translators, by necessity, have been compelled to take considerable license with the source material simply because its old Chinese will not translate literally into English. As evidence, merely witness the great differences in the many conscientious efforts.

The New Lao Tzu, therefore, embraces willingly what translators have admitted reluctantly and employed sparingly. Priority has been given to what is meant rather than what is written, to the spirit of the *Lao Tzu's* teachings rather than the record of its words. Such an approach offers readers in the West a relevance and a clarity that cannot be reached within the constraints of translation. Liberties have been taken with the words to make the wisdom more accessible.

The *Lao Tzu*, in fact, is not as enigmatic as it seems. But translations make it feel foreign and esoteric because they retain too much of the idiom of ancient China. The peculiarities of a uniquely Chinese style of expression make the old classic unnecessarily difficult, and create the impression that its wisdom is somehow remote and obscure.

This does not mean that *The New Lao Tzu* makes this wisdom instantly available. But the first, and perhaps the most extraneous level of difficulty has been removed. What remains is the bare and exposed teachings revealed in clear and simple language.

In China this wisdom is called the Tao. In other places it is given other names. But all those who undertake to search for it experience a similar intellectual and existential crisis as they discover that the same culture that nourishes what they can understand also obstructs what they hope to understand. Indeed, understanding is an impediment that confines insights just as self is a reference that limits knowing. The paradox in Taoism is that the Way can be followed only when it is not understood, and when there is no one to follow it. So the standard measure of progress when searching for its wisdom is a deepening confusion and uncertainty as the impositions of culture and self fall away.

Although the *Lao Tzu* contains individual themes that can be understood as concise and coherent notions, the larger challenge of integrating the entire work into an explainable philosophy is impossible. The interconnections of its diverse and contradictory elements will not intellectually fit together. This is evident in translations, and applies equally to this interpretation. Indeed, no amount of effort will succeed in producing a logical and coherent document that will be understood in a wholly rational way.

The *Lao Tzu* is a gestalt that resembles the paradoxes of life itself. Any honest and thinking person who attempts to grasp its comprehensive wisdom finally reaches a condition in which all intellectual processes collapse. Out of this initial and profound confusion a unique sensitivity develops, a special feeling for the diverse complexity of things as they manifest themselves from moment to moment in the shifting field of a unified wholeness. The wisdom of the *Lao Tzu* does not rest in any answers that it offers, but in its ability to tease confusion into an awareness that is beyond the confinement of intellect's understanding.

Living the wisdom of the *Lao Tzu* requires more instinct than reason, more intuition than argument. So *The New Lao Tzu* is more the work of the poet and the artist than the philosopher and the scholar. It was produced primarily by a creative process, one that remains essentially private and inexplicable.

But this does not excuse accountability. Even the poet's freedom arises from discipline, and the interpreter's liberty must begin with informed preparation. So the scholarly effort that underlies *The New Lao Tzu* must be shared. For those who are interested, it is offered in the several essays that follow the text.

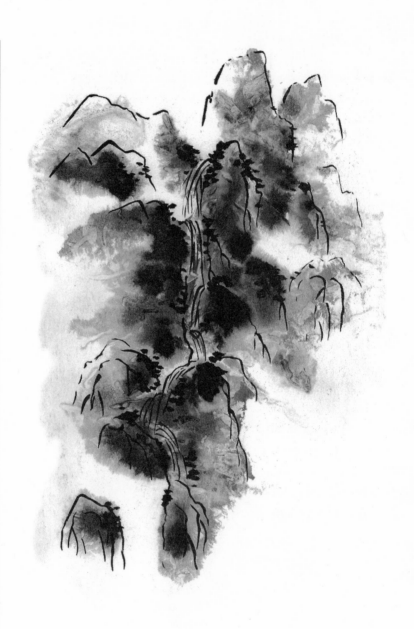

THE CHAPTERS

The age and authority of the recently discovered *Ma-wang-tui* texts require that *The New Lao Tzu* follow its order of chapters. Unfortunately, this order does not correspond to the one in traditional translations.

For readers who are accustomed to the traditional designations, those numbers are always cited to the right of the new number, in smaller type. A conversion can usually be made by adding thirty-seven to those chapters from one to forty-four, and by subtracting forty-four from those chapters numbering forty-five to eighty-one. The following table can be used for a precise conversion.

TE

TAO

The Ma-wang-tui Chapters   The Traditional Chapters

The Ma-wang-tui Chapters	The Traditional Chapters

TE

1 | 38

Virtue that arises from the deepest source
    is unaware of virtue,
  And is one with the Tao.

  Virtue that comes from obligation and pretention
    attempts to be virtuous,
  And is not truly virtuous.

Power that arises from the deepest source
    is unnoticed,
  And cannot be resisted.

  Power that comes from purpose and willfulness
    is apparent,
  And provokes opposition.

When the Tao is lost,
  virtue is taught.
When virtue is lost,
  morality is preached.
When morality is lost,
  propriety is practiced.

  Now propriety is the husk of virtue,
    the seed of suspicion,
  And the beginning of discord.

Without the Tao,
    Kindness and compassion
        are replaced by law and justice;
    Faith and trust are supplanted
        by ritual and ceremony.

    When people become disconnected
        from the inherent simplicity of things,
    They lose their primal virtue.

    And then they invite even more trouble
        by turning to prophets and seers.

Therefore,
    The sage is guided
        by the deep and the unknown;
    By what is,
        rather than what appears to be;
    By inner sense,
        rather than outer show.

⊰⊱

Everything moves in oneness.
   This is why the sky is clear,
      and the earth is solid;
   Why the valleys abound with life,
      and all the living creatures
         grow and flourish.
   Because some things lead and others follow,
      each thing belongs just so.
   And there is even wisdom
      to remember this oneness.

Without the clarity of sky,
   there would be no vision.
Without the solidity of earth,
   there would be no stillness.
Without the life of valleys,
   there would be no nourishment.
Without the living creatures,
   there would be no joy.
Without leaders and followers,
   there would be no order.
Without wisdom,
   there would be no wonder.

Because of wonder,
>The lowest and the highest
>>are joined together in oneness;
>So even the wisest and the most powerful
>>are left silent and subdued,
>>>bewildered and overcome.

>This is why the highest condition
>>of understanding
>Is deep humility
>>and profound confusion.

Therefore,
>The sage does not measure
>>one thing against another.
>And the stone and the jewel
>>are honored as equals.

❖

When the wise hear of the Tao,
   they recognize it.
When the ordinary hear of the Tao,
   they are confused by it.
When the foolish hear of the Tao,
   they laugh at it.
Without the laughter,
   the Tao would not be the Tao.

Thus it is said:
   Understanding the Tao
      is like being confused;
   Finding the Tao
      is like being lost.

The easiest path
   is the most difficult to follow;
The greatest power
   is unnoticed.

The purest is impure;
The best is flawed;
The perfect is imperfect.

The highest virtue is ordinary;
The finest sound is silence;
The largest shape is boundless;
The eternal form is formless.

Therefore,
    The Tao cannot be named,
        cannot be thought or found;
    And yet because of it
        all things are nourished,
    And everything fulfills itself.

4 | 40

The world moves in its own way;
And the sage follows
  by yielding.

The world is known
  by what is;
And what is
  is known by what is not.

From the Tao
  came oneness;
And from oneness
  came twoness.
Then from twoness
  came threeness;
And from threeness
  came everything.

Because the Tao cannot be known
  and oneness cannot be explained,
Opposites and differences
  define and explain each other.
And their shifting balance
  maintains the harmony of things.

Nothing in the world is separate,
  unworthy or lost.
Yet sages call themselves by such names.
Why?
Because losing is a way of finding,
And emptying is a way of filling.
This has been the teaching since ancient times.

. . .

5 | 42

The teaching has also been:
"Those who live by violence
will die by violence."
And this, too,
is taught once again.

⬦

Softness overcomes hardness;
The formless is greater than form.

Therefore,
    The sage does without doing,
    Works without effort,
    Teaches without words.

Which is more important,
fame or contentment?
Which is more valuable,
wealth or integrity?
Which is more useful,
getting or losing?

From possession
comes loss.
From attachment
comes misfortune.

Therefore,
Those who are empty,
remain undisturbed.
And those who master desire,
live to a peaceful end.

Perfection is imperfect
    so the world remains vital.
Fullness is empty
    so the source remains boundless.

Therefore,
    The straightest course wanders;
    The best teaching confuses;
    And the greatest eloquence is wordless.

    In the cold of winter,
        keep moving;
    In the heat of summer,
        be still.

So the sage balances
    the opposites of the world
    By moving with an inner stillness.

When the Tao is followed,
    the war-horses plough fields;
When the Tao is not followed,
    the war-horses ravage countrysides.

The greatest misfortune
    is desire.
The greatest burden
    is greed.
The greatest curse
    is discontent.

Only those who know
    when enough is enough
Will ever have enough.

Without gazing out a window,
    the way of the world can be seen.
Without stepping beyond a door,
    the way of the Tao can be followed.

The Way does not get closer
    by searching farther.

Therefore,
    The sage keeps to the beginning
        to discover the end.
    And finds
        without seeking;
    Arrives
        without leaving;
    Does
        without doing;
    And knows
        without understanding.

⟡

Learning consists of filling;
Following the Tao consists of emptying.

So the sage does less and less
    until nothing is done.
When things are doing themselves,
    nothing is left undone.

To live harmoniously
    in the world,
Let the world do itself.

Selflessly,
    the sage becomes one with others.
  And with an inner emptiness,
    people are received as they are.

The good and the bad
    are accepted,
So acceptance is nourished.

The honest and the dishonest
    are trusted,
So trust is nourished.

Thoughtlessly,
    the sage receives the world as it is.
  And with an inner stillness,
    becomes one with the wholeness of all.

13 | 50

People are born into life,
    and they pass into death.
Between this beginning and end,
    only three people in ten choose the path of life;
Three in ten choose the path of death;
And the rest are so afraid of death
    that they waste life.

Why do people choose the path of death?
    Because they think that death
      has nothing to do with them.
Why are people afraid of death?
    Because they value life too highly.

Those who choose the path of life,
    it is said,
    Meet neither danger nor disaster.
By attending to the world as it is,
    they are untouched by threat or injury.
By avoiding weapons,
    they are untouched by weapons.

Why do these people live so long?
    Because they are at one with life,
      and know all the ways
    That death can enter.

Because of the Tao,
     all things arise from the Great Mother.
She is the body of everything that is.

Each thing is formed from her substance,
     nourished by her generosity,
          sustained in her vitality.

Because the Tao does not control
          or interfere,
Each thing is shaped by its own nature,
     moved by its own purpose,
          fulfilled by its own integrity.
By being itself,
     each thing complies with the Tao.

Why does the greatest power
     and the highest virtue
          not control or interfere?

So that all things
     can be themselves.

The beginning
    is called the Great Mother.
She is the form and the substance
    of the world,
The body of all that is.

    To know the world,
        know the Great Mother;
    To become one with the world,
        become one with the Tao.

    Be caring and attentive,
        and the world is fulfilling;
    Be excessive and reckless,
        and the world is ruthless.

As the brightest comes from the darkest,
    and the greatest comes from the least,
So the Great Mother's wisdom
    comes from the Tao.

To not follow the Tao,
    is the source of misfortune.

The path of the Tao
　　is easy to follow.
Only a little wisdom is needed
　　to walk its ancient and constant way.
But people are easily lured
　　from the safe and the certain
To the narrow and the dangerous.

When luxury and excess begin in high places,
　　the effects spread everywhere.
Soon the cultivated fields are untended,
　　and the country's granaries are empty.

When leaders have more wealth than wisdom,
　　they prefer fancy clothes and exotic foods,
　　　　foolish amusements and self-indulgence.
When they place their own well-being
　　above the care of others,
They are worse than common thieves.

When leaders follow a course of folly,
　　the whole country walks a perilous path.

⬥

The deeply rooted will hold.
The center stillness will last.
Thus from generation to generation,
    the ancient Way endures.

When the Tao is followed:
    Virtue that grows within a person
        will be deep;
    Virtue that grows within a family
        will be genuine;
    Virtue that grows within a community
        will be natural.

When virtue is natural
    it will abound in a nation;
And then it will be abundant
    in the world.

So it is that:
    From a person
        comes a family,
    And from a family
        comes a community;
    From a community
        comes a nation,
    And from a nation
        comes the world.

Therefore,
    The world is changed
        by each person
    Attending to the Tao that is within.

Those who follow the Tao
seem like newborn infants.
Because of an inner stillness,
poisonous snakes are not startled by them;
Wild animals are not threatened by them;
Birds of prey are not attracted by them.

Though their bones are soft
and their muscles are weak,
the grip of the newborn is strong.
Because they are unaware of differences,
their attention is undivided.
Because they do not strain,
they can holler all day
without becoming hoarse.
Why are they able to do these things?
Because they are still at one
with the primal source.

Being at one with the primal source
    comes from following the deepest constant.
Following the deepest constant
    comes from insight.
Insight begins with acceptance.

It is unwise to meddle
    with the way of the world,
To hasten the course of things,
    to go beyond the natural order.
Whatever is not in accord with the Tao,
    will not endure.

Those who know
   cannot explain.
And those who can explain
   do not know.

Therefore,
   Reject teachings.
   Renounce brilliance.
   Abandon ingenuity.
   Forget about words and ideas.
   Empty and follow the ancient path.

For those who are one with the world,
      there are no differences.
Without differences,
      there is no profit or honor,
         no insult or harm.

   Search but the Tao cannot be found.
   Try but the Tao cannot be avoided.
   It cannot be improved or ennobled,
      altered or debased.

Because the Tao is without value,
   it is beyond value.

A country may be governed with justice,
And a war may be won with cunning,
But people can only be mastered
    by following them.

How can this be known?
By looking!
    The more people are controlled,
        the poorer they become;
    The poorer they become,
        the more restless they get;
    The more restless they get,
        the more forcefully they are restrained.

When people are forcefully restrained,
    their defiance becomes ingenious.
And the more ingenious their defiance,
    the stranger are the things that happen.

Now when strange things begin to happen,
    laws and regulations become stricter;
Then stricter laws and regulations
    mean more criminals and fugitives.

. . .

Soon everyone
　　is either a criminal or a fugitive,
And no one can untangle the mess.

Therefore,
　　The sage does nothing
　　　　and people govern themselves,
　　Provokes no one
　　　　and people are peaceful,
　　Does not interfere
　　　　and people prosper,
　　Is without desire
　　　　and people fulfill themselves.

The more people are controlled,
    the less contented they become.
But when will leaders understand
    the significance of this?

Misery is created by bliss,
    and bliss is created by misery.
But who knows when one
    will turn into the other?

Right exists because of wrong,
    and good exists because of bad.
But how long will everyone
    chase these opposites in circles?

Therefore,
    The sage chooses the Tao,
        and follows its way.
    So the path is found
        by leaving it hidden;
    And the world is straightened
        by leaving it crooked.

In leading people
    and in serving the Great Mother,
Less is better than more.

Because the course of least
    is closest to most,
Primal virtue is kept.

With primal virtue,
    great things are possible.
When great things are possible,
    the natural limits are extended;
When the natural limits are extended,
    opportunities open.
To become one with this opening,
    follow the Great Mother's wisdom.

When living roots are deeply set
    in solid ground,
The results are lasting.

Governing a large country
    is like cooking a small fish.

When a country is governed
    according to the Tao,
People are treated gently.

When order is not disturbed,
    disorder does not arise.

When people are not provoked,
    their lives are contented and full.

Because nothing disturbs
    the natural order,
Everything stays in its proper place.

A great nation receives small nations
    like an ocean receives rivers.

By waiting beneath,
    the stillness of the female
Overcomes the male.

By lowering itself,
    a great nation overcomes a small nation.
And by lowering itself,
    a small nation is overcome by a great nation.

Because a great nation
    needs strength and influence,
And a small nation
    needs peace and protection,
Both are fulfilled.

First, however,
    it is incumbent upon the great nation
To lower itself.

All things move in accord with the Tao.
So it is treasure
    to both the good and the bad.

Wealth can be accumulated.
Compliments can be bought and sold.
Honor can be conferred as favor.
But the greatest gift of all
    is ordinary.

When a government is installed
    and its ministers are appointed,
Words of respect and loyalty are pledged.
But the offering that is of highest value
    is the simple wisdom of the Tao.

Why is the Tao so valuable?
    Because it is everywhere,
        and everyone can use it.

. . .

25 | 62

This is why those who seek
 will find,
And those who reform
 will be forgiven;
Why the good
 will be rewarded,
And the thief who is cunning
 will escape.

Because of the Tao,
 all things have a place,
And so the world remains whole.

❖

Trust the natural course of things.
Follow the effortless way.
Taste the tasteless.

Regard the greatest and the least as equals.
Notice the particular.
Be compassionate.

Attend to the easy
    before it becomes difficult.
Cultivate the great
    by nourishing the small.

Great accomplishments are achieved
    through small measures.
The impossible is composed of the possible.

Those without inner direction
    will not be trusted by others.
Those without inner discipline
    will not be favored by the world.

Therefore,
    The sage overcomes difficulty
        by regarding everything as difficult.

Resting things
    are easiest to catch.
Brittle things
    are easiest to break.
Small things
    are easiest to move.
The things that have not yet happened
    are easiest to control.

Deal with problems before they begin.
Cultivate harmony before discord arises.

Huge trees grow from tiny seeds.
Tall buildings start at the ground.
Great heights are reached by single steps.

Since failure is closest
    when success is nearest,
Care and patience are increased
    as endings approach.

However,
    All those who do,
        finally fail;
    And all those who possess,
        finally lose.

Therefore,
    The sage does nothing
        so nothing is left undone;
    And possesses nothing
        so nothing is lost.

Because the sage neither desires nor possesses,
        burdens are not accumulated.
Without burdens,
        an ordered grace unfolds.
By trusting and opening,
        by releasing and attending,
The Way is followed.

When nothing is forced
        and everything is doing itself,
The Tao is revealed.

The ancient sages seemed ordinary
    because they cultivated the wisdom
        of simplicity.

They never told people of the Tao
    because cleverness
        just provokes more cleverness.
And too much cleverness
    creates nothing but trouble.

Those who are clever
    are the thieves of tranquillity;
Those who are simple
    are the guardians of harmony.

Knowing the difference
    between cleverness and simplicity
Is the beginning of wisdom.

⊰◈⊱

Rivers are greater than streams
    because they are below them;
Oceans are greater than rivers
    because they are below them.

Therefore,
    The sage rises above
        by staying below;
    And stays ahead
        by remaining behind.

When above is below
    and ahead is behind,
Nothing in the world
    is overpowered or overtaken.

So the sage serves with humility
    but does not lead,
And everything follows
    its own harmonious course.

Because the sage does not oppose,
    opposition is not provoked;
Because the sage does not resist,
    resistance is not created.

A small country with a few people
is better than a large country
with many people.

Why is this so?
Because people in small countries
remain simple:
They stay home.
They honor life.
They respect death.
They tend to their own affairs.
And they arm only for defense.

Large countries display their might;
Small countries live their humility.

In small countries,
people are uncomplicated:
They enjoy their food.
They take pride in themselves.
They maintain their customs.
They appreciate their homes.
And they value contentment.

Because small countries
are ordinary,
They are good neighbors.

❦

Simple words
    are the most profound;
And the most profound words
    are simple.

People who argue
    do not understand;
And people who understand
    do not argue.

Those who have something to defend
    are not wise;
And those who are wise
    have nothing to defend.

Therefore,
    The sage empties
        and is filled;
    Gives
        and is enriched;
    Yields
        and is fulfilled;
    Follows the wisdom of the Tao
        and becomes the grace of the world.

Those who know of the Tao
    recognize it as great.

Why is it great?
Because it is different.

Why is it different?
Because it cannot be understood.
If it could be understood,
    it would not have lasted
        from the beginning of the beginning.

There are three treasures to keep:
        Compassion,
        Simplicity,
        Humility.

From compassion comes strength.
From simplicity comes insight.
From humility comes influence.

Without compassion,
     strength becomes cruelty;
Without simplicity,
     insight becomes confusion;
Without humility,
     influence becomes tyranny.

Of these three treasures,
     It is compassion
          that softens the hardness in the world.
     So compassion is the softness
          that strengthens the sage.

The best leaders
    are never reckless;
The best fighters
    are never angry.

Not even victory justifies revenge;
Not even power excuses pride.

The greatest power
    exercises no power.
The greatest strength
    arises from humility.
The greatest virtue
    follows the way of the Tao.

In times of war,
> be guided by these principles:
Cunning is better than force;
Attacking is preferable to being attacked;
Strategic retreats are favored
> above costly advances.

In the art of war
> cultivate these tactics:
Move forward without appearing to advance,
> without revealing either strength or weakness;
Engage the enemy without confronting them,
> without meeting them in open battle.

The greatest mistake
> is underestimating the enemy.
The greatest misfortune
> is forgetting the gravity of war.

Therefore,
The winners will be those
> who are in accord with the Tao.

❖

These words are easy to understand,
    and these teachings are easy to follow.
But no one understands the words,
    and no one follows the teachings.

These words follow a principle,
    and the world has an order.
But no one understands the principle,

Because no one recognizes
    the inner wisdom of things,
The sage is mistaken for the fool.

The wise know
    they do not know;
The fools do not know
    they do not know.

Those who recognize
      the ignorance in ignorance
    Are not ignorant;
And those who recognize
      the foolishness in foolishness
    Are not foolish.

Therefore,
    By knowing
      both ignorance and foolishness,
    The sage becomes wise.

When force is used frequently,
    people stop fearing it.
Then trouble begins.

So the sage avoids trouble
    by avoiding force.

When force is not used,
    people do not resist.
What is not resisted,
    cannot be opposed.

Therefore,
    The sage relies on the hidden
        rather than the apparent;
    Trusts the inner
        rather than the outer.
    And by doing nothing,
        order maintains itself.

Those who are fearless and disciplined
    are favored by the world;
Those who are fearless and undisciplined
    are not favored by the world.

Some things are in accord
    with the Tao.
    Some things are not.
    But no one knows why.

Following the Tao
    is disciplined yet easy.
The way is dark and profound,
    wordless and silent.

Although the Tao seems indifferent
    and aimless,
    Its course is precise and unerring.

The Tao is like a vast net.
    Although its mesh is too large
        to be found,
    Nothing can escape it.

❖

If people are not afraid of dying,
    they cannot be threatened with death.
If people are afraid of dying,
    who is qualified to kill them?

Death is always waiting,
    but who dares
To be the executioner?

Therefore,
    Those who try to carve wood
        like a master,
    Invariably cut themselves.

Why are poor people hungry?
Because their poverty
    is not the concern of rich people.

Why are simple people restless?
Because their peace
    has been disturbed by complicated people.

Why do so many people care so little about dying?
Because a few people
    care too much about living.

When there is little of value in life,
    people are not afraid of death.

People at birth
    are soft and supple;
At death,
    they are hard and stiff.

When plants are alive,
    they are green and bending;
When they are dead,
    they are dry and brittle.

Soft and bending is the way of the living;
Hard and brittle is the way of the dying.

Therefore,
    A great strength
        that is inflexible,
    Will break in the wind
        like an old dead tree.

So the arrogant and the unyielding
    will fall;
And the humble and the yielding
    will overcome.

The way of the Tao
>is like the bending of a bow:
As the bow is pulled,
>the top lowers and the bottom rises.
Because the ends are connected,
>the extremes are reduced.

If the string is too long,
>it is shortened;
If the string is too short,
>it is lengthened.

Such is the way of nature;
It decreases what is too much,
>and it increases what is too little.

But this is not the way of people;
>Those who have too much
>>take even more;
And those who have too little
>>get even less.

. . .

So the sage returns
to the natural balance.

How is this done?
By having
without possessing.
By doing
without expecting.
By being
without desiring.

❦

The softness of water
    erodes the hardness of stone.
Yielding overcomes unyielding.
The weak outlast the strong.
Those who bend
    endure long after the unbending have
       broken.

This is known by many,
    but practiced by few.

Therefore,
    The sage embraces humility,
       and honors the way of the Tao;
    Lives close to the earth,
       and welcomes its bitterness.

So it is that the lowest
    become the highest;
And the least
    become the greatest.

Even after a great conflict
        has been resolved,
    Resentment remains.

    Such resentment
            is the source of new trouble.

Therefore,
    It is unwise
            to provoke the loser,
    To make demands
            and assign guilt.

Those who forget grievances
nourish peace;
And those who remember grievances
perpetuate discord.

Because the Tao is impartial,
those who follow the Tao
Are also impartial.
Thus balance is restored
by those with balance.

TAO

45 | 1

The Tao that can be named
  is not the nameless Tao.
The Tao that can be known
  is not the unknowable Tao.

Nameless and unknowable,
    the Tao has been from the very beginning.
It is the wisdom of all that is,
    and the way of the Great Mother.

With desire,
    the Tao is hidden.
Without desire,
    the Tao is apparent.

The Tao and the Great Mother
    arose from the same dark source.
Their names are different,
    but they are inseparable.

Together they are an endless wonder,
And the boundless mystery
    of everything's oneness.

When beauty is recognized as beauty,
    ugliness is created.
When good is recognized as good,
    bad is created.

Front and back
    arise from each other.
Difficult and easy
    determine each other.
High and low
    define each other.
Long and short
    measure each other.
Sound and silence
    echo each other.
Being and non-being
    are each other.

. . .

When the harmony of oneness
    is not disturbed,
All things rise and fall
    in their natural rhythms,
Nourishing and fulfilling themselves
    in graceful order.

Therefore,
    The sage does without doing,
        and teaches without teaching.
    So when great things are accomplished,
        credit is neither given nor taken.
    When tasks are completed,
        they are forgotten.

Because nothing is done,
    no recognition is received.
Because nothing is gained,
    nothing is lost.

Praise
  creates rivalry.
Valuables
  create thieves.
Desire
  creates discontent.

Therefore,
  The sage nurtures accord
    by balancing extremes.

So understanding
  is guided by simplicity.
Ambition
  is tempered by humility.
And strength
  is restrained by compassion.

. . .

47 | 3

When people have nothing to struggle against,
    they do not struggle.
When their contentment is not disturbed,
    they maintain a peaceful order.
When everything seems ordinary,
    the Tao is manifest.

The Tao is like an empty vessel
    that cannot be filled.
Because it is forever empty,
    it is forever useful.

It dulls the sharpened
    and untangles the knotted,
It subdues the brilliant
    and lowers the highest.

Like deep water
    that is dark and still,
The Tao seems unfathomable
    yet eternally present.

Since it has been from the beginning
    of the very beginning,
No one knows how it came to be.

49 | 5

The universe
     does not make exceptions.
Because it is impartial,
     the sage is also impartial.

The universe
     seems to be like a bellows,
And everything is charged by its moving.

The emptiness within
     changes shape but never form.
The more it moves
     the more things happen.

Because words will never explain
     why everything happens,
And thoughts will never understand
     why everything is,
The sage attends to the peaceful stillness
     of an inner balance.

⬦

The mystery of the valley
    is female.
It is the emptiness in woman
    and the fullness of the Great Mother,
The endless source of everything
    and the generosity of all that is.

Although hidden,
    it is everywhere.

To enter it,
    simply empty.

Be used by it,
    and it will not fail.

That which has no beginning
   has no end.
That which is not born
   does not die.
That which is formless
   cannot be destroyed.

Therefore,
   The sage is ahead
      by being behind;
   Is first
      by being last;
   Is whole
      by being empty;
   And is fulfilled
      by being selfless.

Water is like the highest good
    because it flows to the lowest places.
While people strive to move upward,
    water goes freely downward,
And on its effortless course
    nourishes everything in its path.
Such is the way of the Tao.

Therefore,
    Live close to the land.
    Think deeply.
    Be gentle and caring.
    With others,
        be honest and just.
    In business,
        be efficient.
    Attend to details.
    In all situations,
        timing is crucial.

When there is no struggle,
    the natural order is not disturbed.

A bow pulled too far
   will break.
A blade oversharpened
   will not hold an edge.
Hoarded wealth
   cannot be protected.
Honor
   is the source of disgrace.

Therefore,
   The sage is particularly careful
   with endings.

When inner and outer
    move as one,
The harmony of wholeness is experienced.

When hardness and softness
    become the same,
The wisdom of the child is realized.

When living and dying
    are no longer different,
The nourishing female is discovered.

When thoughts
    are finally still,
The way of the world is revealed.

When the Tao is followed,
    Its ancient wisdom is unknowingly practiced.

So nourish the world,
    but do not control it.
Be in the world,
    but do not possess it.

These are the ways of deepest virtue.

Thirty spokes converge in a single hub;
It is the center hole
    that allows the wheel to turn.

A bowl is shaped from clay;
But its usefulness
    comes from the space within.

Doors and windows
    are openings in walls.

And a room can only be used
    because it contains emptiness.

Therefore,
    What is
        is made useful
    By what is not.

The clarity of seeing
    is blinded by bright colors.
The sharpness of hearing
    is dulled by loud sounds.
The keenness of tasting
    is overcome by rich flavors.

Indulging the senses
    interferes with insight.
Precious things
    are distracting.

Therefore,
    The sage is guided by the subtle,
        rather than the conspicuous;
    By what is inside,
        rather than what is outside.

Accept disgrace as the condition of self.
Accept misfortune as the condition of life.

What is meant by,
　　"Accept disgrace
　　　　as the condition of self?"
It means that self is unimportant;
That anyone who gains a self,
　　finally loses a self.
What then is the value
　　of vanity and pride?

What is meant by,
　　"Accept misfortune
　　　　as the condition of life?"
It means that misfortune comes from being alive;
That anyone who is living,
　　finally dies.
What then is the value
　　of wealth and honor?

Therefore,
Those who know the value
of vanity and pride
Can be entrusted with leadership.

And those who know the value
of wealth and honor
Can be entrusted with the world.

Look but it cannot be seen,
    so it has no form.
Listen but it cannot be heard,
    so it makes no sound.
Think but it cannot be thought,
    so it defies understanding.

Because it cannot be discerned,
    it cannot be discovered.
Because it cannot be thought,
    it cannot be known.
Still it seems to be something,
    a something that is everywhere
    but nowhere.

Neither bright nor dark,
    it is described as subtle;
Too subtle
    to be named,
Too near
    to be found.

It seems to be a timeless and unbroken wholeness
    that connects everything to everything else;
Like a shapeless shape
    that is something yet somehow nothing;
Like a nameless secret
    that is forever hidden and unknowable.
Search
    but it has no beginning;
Follow
    but it has no end.

From day to passing day
    it seems to be a constant
        that is worthy of trust;
An endless and eternal thread
    that stretches from the beginning
        of the beginning
To this very moment.

The ancient sages
    were said to be wise and mysterious,
Too subtle to be explained,
    and too profound to be understood.

Since they could neither be explained
    nor understood,
They could only be described.

They seemed:
    Intent
        as if fording a flooding stream;
    Alert
        as if in great danger.

They seemed:
    Respectful
        as courteous guests;
    Yielding
        as melting ice;
    Solid
        as an uncarved block;
    Receptive
        as a broad valley;
    Easy
        as a flowing river.

Amid confusion,
    they seemed to have a clarity;
Amid turmoil,
    they seemed to be peaceful.
When action was required,
    they seemed to wait quietly
        for the perfect moment.

Since they did not fulfill themselves,
    they seemed forever empty,
And unmoved by desire.

❖

Empty until there is only emptiness
   within stillness.
Then selflessly watch the eternal rhythms
   of all things
Rising and falling with themselves.

Each thing becomes and grows and fulfills itself,
   and then returns to its nameless beginning.
Such is the way of all things.

With self still and empty,
   discover the unchanging in all changing.
Knowing this
   leads to wisdom.
Not knowing this
   leads to misfortune.

With wisdom comes tranquillity;
With tranquillity comes softening;
With softening
   the inside self becomes the outside world.
This is the way to the Tao.

Then everything moves
   in timeless balance and harmony,
Peacefully fulfilling itself.

The best leaders
    are hardly noticed.
The next best
    are loved and praised.
Then come those
    who are feared.
And finally those
    who are ridiculed.

Leaders who do not trust
    will not be trusted.

The best doing
    does itself.

Therefore,
    When a great leader
        accomplishes anything,
    Everyone thinks
        it just happened naturally.

When the Tao
     is no longer followed,
Propriety and virtue arise.
Then comes knowledge.
And then ingenuity.
And finally cunning and hypocrisy.

From conflict,
     loyalty arises.
From disaster,
     heroes appear.

Without saints and sages,
    everyone would benefit a hundredfold.

Without propriety and righteousness,
    people would be their natural selves.

Without profit and ingenuity,
    there would be no swindlers and thieves.

Therefore,
    Be guided by these teachings:
        Forget wisdom;
        Honor simplicity;
        Temper desire;
        Abandon self;
        Return to the formless.

Proprieties by the thousands
    control what people do.
But how many of them are really necessary?
Is there very much difference
    between approval and disapproval?
Between proper and improper?
Why must one person do
    what everyone else does?
What nonsense!

At all the appropriate holidays and celebrations
    everyone enthusiastically participates.
At the proper times they go to the proper places,
    and eagerly do the proper things.
How can anyone who just drifts and wonders,
    who can't even be sure of themselves,
Take seriously all these rituals,
    all this herding?
It seems better just to be alone and quiet,
    not belonging anywhere.

Everyone else seems eager and dutiful,
    but the deeper way seems lonely and confusing.
Everyone else seems clear and definite,
    but the deeper way seems dark and uncertain.

What is a person to do when being adrift at sea,
when being blown aimlessly anywhere,
seems to be a more profound calling?
When everyone else seems busy and purposeful,
what is to be done with an urge
that is confusing and lonely,
and different?
When everyone else
is guided by the affairs of people,
What is this urge
that comes from the Great Mother?

When the Tao is followed,
    power and virtue become one.
Find the way that is elusive and unknowable,
    effortless and everywhere.

Although the Tao is called by a name,
    it is nameless and mysterious;
Although the Tao is natural and ordinary,
    it is formless and intangible.

Being formless,
    it gives order to the things that happen;
Being intangible,
    it gives substance to the things that are.

Because it is elusive and unknowable,
    it cannot be thought or understood.
Because it is natural and ordinary,
    it can be used and trusted.

Since words have named what cannot be named,
    the Tao seems to be something.
But it is a mystery;
A mystery within a mystery
    that is forever hidden yet present,
An inner urge
    that courses through the nature of
        everything.

How can all this be known?
    Because of what is.

66 | 24

Those who stand on tiptoe
   cannot maintain their balance.
Those who hurry
   cannot sustain their pace.

Those who boast
   will not be honored.
Those who brag
   will not be trusted.
Those who are proud
   will not understand.

Such behaviors are called
   "excess food and baggage."
So those who follow the Tao
   do not need them.

By yielding,
    overcome.
By bending,
    remain straight.
By emptying,
    be filled.
By breaking,
    become whole.
By losing,
    gain.

By following the Tao,
    the sage becomes one with the world.

Therefore,
    Choose emptiness
        to find fullness;
    Embrace the formless
        to master form;
    Practice humility
        to attain greatness;
    Claim nothing
        to receive the bounty of the world.

. . .

67 | 22

Because the sage does not struggle
     with the world,
The world does not resist.

An ancient teaching says,
     "A winding path reaches its destination."
By yielding to the way of the world,
     the sage is fulfilled by the world.

❖

The sage rarely uses force.
    Why?
Because high winds and heavy rains
    last only a short while.
When not even the Great Mother
    can sustain the power of storms,
What can mere people do
    with their petty outbursts?

Those who use force
    soon exhaust themselves.
And what can be accomplished
    with exhaustion and struggle?

But those who follow the Tao
    become one with the Tao.
Because they move with the world,
    they become one with the force of its moving.
Because they are one with the world,
    great things happen easily.

Therefore,
    Those who trust
        the way of the world
    Are empowered by the world.

Out of a dark chaos
    came something unknowable and unchanging;
Something silent and formless and vast,
    alone and mysterious.

Because this mystery cannot be known or named,
    it is called the Tao.
Words describe it as great
    because it seems to go on and on,
Endlessly and forever turning with itself.

To know the world,
    return to the Tao.
It is the source
    of deepest wisdom.

There are four great powers to consider:
The Tao,
The way of nature,
The workings of the world,
The affairs of people.

People conduct themselves
    according to the world.
The world conducts itself
    according to nature.
Nature conducts itself
    according to the Tao.
The Tao conducts itself
    according to itself.

Proper lightness
    springs from the root of heaviness.
Proper action
    springs from the root of stillness.

If a traveller can remain calm and peaceful
    throughout the ordeals of an arduous journey,
Then how much more is required of a leader
    in the heat of a crisis?

Without heaviness,
    lightness is frivolous.
Without stillness,
    action is impetuous.

The best walking
    leaves no footprints.
The best words
    leave nothing unsaid.
The best calculations
    make no mistakes.

The best locks cannot be opened
    because they use no bolts or bars.
The best knots cannot be untied
    because they use no ropes or cords.

Therefore,
    The sage guides
        by giving no direction;
    And leads
        by following.

. . .

Because oneness is everywhere,
Everything is sustained and balanced
by an inherent wisdom.
Thus good people are occupied
reforming bad people;
And those who think they know,
teach those who think they do not know.
Because respect and order are valued,
people control themselves.
Because they find their own way,
they are contented and fulfilled.

So the sage follows
the wisdom of oneness,
And merely does
what happens naturally.

Know the strength of the masculine
 but cultivate the care of the feminine,
And become the living valley.
As the living valley,
 be close to the Tao
And return to the primal beginning.

Know the brightness of the light
 but honor the wisdom of the dark,
And become the living mystery.
As the living mystery,
 enter the nature of the world
And return to the Great Mother.

Know the perfection of the highest
 but follow the humility of the lowest,
And become the living stream.
As the living stream,
 flow to the deepest places
And return to primal simplicity.

In primal simplicity,
 the things of the world nourish themselves;
Because everything rises and falls
 in harmonious accord,
Nothing needs to be changed.

Those who try to improve the world
    will not succeed.
Those who try to control it
    will ruin it.
And those who try to possess it
    will lose it.

The world is its own place,
    and has its own ways:
So some things are ahead
    because others are behind;
Some things are still
    because others are moving;
Some things are strong
    because others are weak;
And some things are new
    because others are old.

Therefore,
    The sage embraces the opposites
        of the world,
    And with an inner balance
        enters a greater wisdom.

Force creates resistance.
Because those who follow the Tao
    do not use force,
Force is not used against them.

Where armies arise
    there is deprivation;
Where armies pass
    there is devastation.

When doing arises of itself,
    it creates no resistance.

Therefore,
    When results are achieved:
        There is no glory in victory,
        No pride in success,
        No arrogance in fame,
        No reward in profit.

Because force is the beginning of failure,
    those who use it
Are finally undone by their own doing.

The best weapons
    are the most feared
Because they cause
    the greatest destruction.

Therefore,
    The sage avoids using them.

    Favor is given to the left hand
        of gentleness
    Rather than the right hand
        of force.

    Since weapons are instruments of misfortune,
        they are used only as a last resort;
    Peace and tranquillity are honored above
        contention and war.

Since the celebration of victory
    is also the celebration of killing,
A victory is not an occasion for joy,
    but for mourning.

    With so many dead,
        a victory should be observed
    With the rites of a funeral.

Although the Tao is simple,
    it cannot be explained.
Because it cannot be explained,
    no one can understand it.
If people would follow
    its simple way,
The natural rhythms of all things
    would rise and fall in easy order.

But thinking has divided
    the wholeness of things,
Invented systems
    and given names to parts.
Now there are systems for everything,
    too many parts to count,
And no one knows
    when the dividing will stop.

. . .

Knowing when to stop
    is the best way of avoiding trouble.

Following the Tao
    Is like the valley stream
        joining a great river,
    And flowing peacefully to the sea.

❖

Knowing others
    is understanding;
Knowing self
    is wisdom.

Force can master others,
    but only strength can master self.

Contentment is wealth,
    and serenity is treasure.

Therefore,
    Renounce outer force
        and be at ease with the world.
    Cultivate inner strength
        and trust the enduring center.
    Expect a long life
        and die fulfilled.

The Tao is everywhere.
It nourishes everything
    yet it controls nothing.

Because it controls nothing,
    it seems unimportant;
Because it nourishes everything,
    it is valued beyond value.

Because it is ordinary,
    it seems worthless;
Because it is everywhere,
    it is called great.

Because it does not claim greatness,
    its greatness is even greater.

The form that endures forever
    is without form.
So those who follow the formless
    find comfort and peace and fulfillment.

Being formless,
    the Tao is everywhere.
Being everywhere,
    it is hardly noticed.
Because it is hardly noticed,
    it is ordinary.
Because it is ordinary,
    it offers the deepest nourishment.

Therefore,
    Be nourished by what cannot be seen
        or heard or found.
    It is inexhaustible.

Increasing
    is followed by decreasing;
Gaining
    is followed by losing;
Rising
    is followed by falling;
Acceptance
    is followed by rejection;
Strengthening
    is followed by weakening.

This is why softness and weakness
    overcome hardness and strength.

Therefore,
    A fish
        should not stray from deep water;
    And power
        should not be displayed.

The Tao cannot be named,
    cannot be known,
    Yet its wisdom can be followed.

If people would follow this wisdom,
    they would not disturb
    The natural order of things.

But if people must have their own way,
    let them be guided
      by nameless simplicity.
Thus they will be content,
    and their actions will arise
      without desire.

And without their desire,
    the natural order
      will fulfill itself.

THE
ESSAYS

THE
TRANSLATION
PROBLEM

A new English translation of the *Lao Tzu* has appeared about once every two years since the first version by John Chalmers in 1868.[1] But the many variations in these versions suggest that the old classic cannot be translated, at least not in the usual sense in which the term is understood.

Translators of the *Lao Tzu* have been confronted with the daunting task of constructing an English version from a number of traditional Chinese texts, each different, and each to varying degrees incomplete, incorrect, disjointed, obscure, illegible, and deliberately adulterated. In many places even the Chinese themselves can can only surmise the meaning of the texts. And then translators face the Chinese language itself, a language that has no direct structural correspondence with English.

To these two fundamental obstacles, translators of the *Lao Tzu* meet a style that employs subtlety, ambiguity, and paradox. Some passages are playfully exaggerated and convoluted. Some suggest rather than explain. Others seem to be expressions of unbridled poetic license. These attributes compound the difficulty of producing an accurate translation.

Consider, for example, the first twelve characters of the Tao section of the text. *The New Lao Tzu* renders them as:

> The Tao that can be named
> is not the nameless Tao.
> The Tao that can be known
> is not the unknowable Tao.

In each of the nine translations that have been used to guide this interpretation, these same twelve characters have been translated so differently that some versions only remotely resemble others. In *Tao: The Watercourse Way*, Alan Watts cites six more translations, each different from the nine already counted.

Although this is a somewhat extreme example of the kind of difficulties that occur throughout the *Lao Tzu*, it illustrates that translation cannot be separated from understanding, a statement that in other circumstances would be too self-evident to mention. Holmes Welch summarizes this problem when he writes in *Taoism: The Parting of the Way*, "To read is an act of creation."[2] Translating the *Lao Tzu* is so difficult that intelligent guessing rather than translating is often the rule rather than the exception.

Some of this difficulty is rooted in the inherent ambiguity of the Chinese written language itself. Because Chinese writing developed as a mnemonic device that did not evolve by borrowing significantly from other sources, a limited number of symbols eventually had to represent an increasing number of meanings.[3] Consequently, the range of meanings for any one character grew greater and greater until the communicative accuracy of the language began to collapse. Too often in ancient China the meaning of a character had to be guessed by its context. If the context was not clear or the intended meaning was no longer remembered, the passage could not be understood. To make the writing more precise, additional characters called radicals were added alongside the primary one, but this was never practiced regularly or adequately until the third century B.C.[4] Even in modern Chinese this problem of ambiguity still exists. The written language continues to bear remnants of its mnemonic origin, and unless the reader remembers the meaning or is able to deduce it from the larger context, some characters are still ambiguous.

Translations are thwarted by another matter. Although the *Lao Tzu* is interspersed with clear and unambiguous images, with earthy and practical advice that is offered with the logical reasoning of the philosopher, its real subject lies outside the domain of words and is not amenable to any explanation. The most important insights in the *Lao Tzu* can be only glimpsed, hinted at rather than stated. The essential and deepest meanings reside between the words, in the outside spaces that escape explanation. Like Keats's Grecian urn, the words "tease us out of thought as doth eternity." The words nurture insights that are subtle and elusive, that are reached by cultivated intuition rather than rational construction. Often described in the negative, these insights drift like gossamers beyond the reach of definition and articulation. The words cast shadows rather than substance, indistinct and indescribable shapes that can be sensed but cannot be conceptually grasped. So the translator must somehow hint at their presence, suggest the unsayable, point to what cannot be declared.

Herein lies the opening that allows the particular personal and cultural disposition of the translator to be projected into the text. So with every additional translation, the *Lao Tzu* is transformed into another shape with a different meaning. Some translations remain comfortably Taoist; others have overtones that are conspicuously Platonic, some even Christian, as these philosophies are implanted into a literature that is uniquely Chinese. Other translations seem impossibly enigmatic—virtually indecipherable—as the wonderful wholeness of a subtle but essentially simple teaching is broken into confusion by passing through the prism of English.

But not all the confusion can be attributed to the refractive effects of translation. The *Lao Tzu* has a logic of its own that does not pass easily into the philosophy of the West. It is a strict aesthetic conducted with a disciplined softness in an atmosphere of deliberate ambiguity. The consequence is a way of understanding that is impossible to convey within the framework of reasoned definition; the process is closer to the dynamics of art than the clarity of explanation.

Taoism, like Zen, is not a philosophy of life; it is the art of being. Like the artistic process itself, Taoism embraces all the inherent contradictions of living, and then it converts the creative energy that results from this tension into a balancing and harmonizing experience. How this happens cannot be explained. Its deepest insights cannot be expressed in straight answers. These insights at the core of Taoism are utterly and wonderfully perplexing—and exactly right. So the translator of the *Lao Tzu* must somehow follow a crooked path to deepest understanding, must clearly say what can be said to suggest what cannot be said.

But another formidable problem for translators still exists. This is simply the disjointed nature of the *Lao Tzu* itself. Between clearly expressed ideas are empty spaces that must also be read, understood, and reproduced. They, too, must be translated. When conventional patterns of linear thinking meet such discontinuity, they are forced to make creative leaps. With the proper momentum, these leaps can lead to an awakening that is fresh and timeless, to an intuitive insightfulness that offers a perpetual readiness. But the style of writing that opens to this condition also disrupts the line of thinking that gives guidance to the translator. The same process that challenges thinking and inspires deep wisdom is also the obstacle that makes translating nearly impossible.

Translators must also account for the lack of equivalence between the characters of old Chinese and the words of modern English. Consider the apparently simple task of finding an English equivalent for the *te* that appears about forty-four times in the *Lao Tzu*.

Te is usually translated as virtue. But virtue in the West is a word too imbued with moralistic and judgmental overtones to be understood in the philosophically amoral way that is intended in the *Lao Tzu*. *Te* is clearly not to be understood in a narrowly moral or ethical sense, although it has been twisted in this direction by a Confucian influence. Sometimes *te* is translated as power, even character—that quality which gives each thing its distinctive integrity, its individual identity. Since character often manifests itself as power, *te* can probably be understood as a combination of virtue and power, as virtue-power.

But this meaning raises other complications. To think of *te* as a noun is misleading because it does not fit comfortably into that grammatical category. It is not so much a noun as a verb. As a verb it is passive rather than active. *Te* is also somewhat gerundial, a verb that is used as a noun. But it is also adjectival, an attribute.

Perhaps te can be most clearly understood when it is thought of in terms of concrete Chinese pragmatism rather than grammatical or philosophical notions. Taoism, like Zen, is particularly interested in spontaneous action, in the kind of doing that arises intuitively when the inner self is connected directly to the outer world. Inner awareness, therefore, is justified only through manifest consequences, when the so-called self abandons its willfulness and learns to function synchronistically with the world's natural unfolding, when individual doing becomes an integral part of the unfolding whole. Inner discovery thereby becomes outer process. Individual behavior is no longer guided by willfulness but by a deep empathy with everything else, an empathy that precludes any personal opposition to the larger way of things. This is the virtue component of virtue-power. It is not derived from moral goodness. Indeed, moral goodness is derived from it.

And what of the power component of virtue-power? By moving within the context of wholeness, power just happens. But it has no control over anything. It is experienced as a grace that arises spontaneously out of the harmonious relationship of the self with the larger unfolding. The power is the virtue; they are the same thing. How is such a concept to be translated when it has no literal or philosophical equivalent in English?

Translators meet a comparable problem with cultural allusions that are exclusive to ancient China. These allusions appear frequently in the *Lao Tzu*, and are usually used metaphorically to express an idea by implied comparison. If a reader in the modern West does not have a literal understanding of these allusions because they are obscure, then they cannot be understood at the metaphorical level. Scholarly explanation will alleviate some of this obscurity but it will not eliminate the sense of cultural distance that separates the *Lao Tzu* from those who are reading it in translation. The reader is still required to think in Chinese images, to approach as a foreigner a wisdom that should feel immediate and familiar.

If these obstacles are not enough to confound the translator, then there is old Chinese itself, perhaps the greatest obstacle of all. As Holmes Welch points out, this problem is virtually insurmountable.[5] Imagine translating from a language that has no singular or plural, no active or passive voice, no case, no person, no mood, and no tense. It has no definite or indefinite articles. All its rules are flexible. Almost any character can be used as any part of speech. Sometimes, as a kind of shorthand, the radical of a character is deleted; the result, according to Welch, is like writing only "ization" instead of "civilization." Whenever possible the subject of a sentence is omitted. Conjunctions are rarely used, so the translator must surmise how two ideas that appear together are logically related. These formidable challenges to translation are increased by a nearly total absence of punctuation. As a written language Chinese is fundamentally vague. And the subtle, complex, poetic, and paradoxical attributes of the *Lao Tzu* compound the effects.

This vagueness was such an accepted part of the Chinese literary tradition, explains Welch,[6] that they dealt with it by providing commentaries that explained the classics. More than 1,500 volumes were written for the *Lao Tzu* alone. Then, these were often followed by subcommentaries that explained the commentaries or further explained the texts. This system was required not because the literature was necessarily difficult, but because the written language was vague.

Written Chinese also has a condensed quality that invites vagueness. This imprecision is amplified by the particularly condensed poetic style of the *Lao Tzu* itself. The effect is somewhat like reading and writing in telegrams of free verse.

To this source of potential confusion, add the rich and expansive nature of each individual, written character. The result is a wealth of suggestion that lacks the guidance of structure, a perfect combination for misunderstanding.

All these difficulties in translating the *Lao Tzu* do not even account for the errors, omissions, and obscurities that have been created as the source material has been copied and recopied over the centuries. There is no extant, original version of the *Lao Tzu*. Of the traditional texts that do exist, most scholars now agree that some of the characters are incorrect and the meanings of others are uncertain. Still other characters—indeed, whole lines of them—are incorrectly placed. And some characters and lines are missing entirely. This has been confirmed by the recently discovered *Ma-wang-tui* texts, which have filled in as many as three missing lines in one so-called chapter.

The traditional *Lao Tzu* texts have also been contaminated by copying errors. Some were made inadvertently, as transcribers simply forgot or misread characters, or even made incorrect corrections. Other errors were made deliberately as scholars—most likely Confucians—adjusted the Taoist texts to accommodate their own particular purposes. Commentaries were added that then became indistinguishable from the parent texts. Translators who have been working from such modified versions have been under the considerable handicap of using adulterated, incomplete, and inaccurate source material.

Not counting the recently discovered *Ma-wang-tui* texts, at least six Chinese versions of the *Lao*

Tzu exist, each with variations. Although the book is commonly known in China as *The Classic of Five Thousand Characters*, the count of these characters, as Victor H. Mair points out, ranges from 5,227 to 5,722.[7]

Of these Chinese versions of the *Lao Tzu*—the *Wang Pi, Ching Lung, Wu Ch'en, Ho Shang Kung, Wei Yuan*,[8] and *Yen Tsun*[9]—the oldest is attributed to Yen Tsun from the first century B.C., although this version exists as a copy of at least another copy. The *Ho Shang Kung* is said to be from the third century B.C. but this claim is questionable—it is probably from six hundred years later.[10] Waley ascribes the oldest to Wang Pi.[11]

The version assigned to Wang Pi (A.D. 226 –249) is believed to be one of the most reliable of the traditional texts, and later ones are considered to be variants of it. The authority of the *Wang Pi*, however, is based upon its close agreement with the *Ho Shang Kung*. But the reputability of the *Ho Shang Kung* is questionable. In all cases, however, no original manuscripts exist, only the received texts that have been copied and perhaps re-copied numerous times over the centuries. Between the historical origin of Taoism and the oldest existing edition of its traditional texts, centuries of unknown changes have been made. There is no original manuscript by Lao Tzu, and in all cases the texts that are available are to varying degrees both incomplete and inaccurate. The *Ma-wang-tui* texts are only partly exempt from these problems.

Yet another major problem for translators must be mentioned. Classical Chinese, the form in which the various versions of the *Lao Tzu* are recorded, is simply long columns of uninterrupted characters with no indication of chapters, stanza/paragraphs, or even sentences.[12] Sentences are determined by what appears to be meaningful units of thought. The present chapter divisions have simply evolved by convention. There is no textual basis for dividing them as they are; the stanza/paragraphs are still discretionary, even in modern Chinese. For translators and readers alike, the meaning of the text is undoubtedly influenced by these divisions.

To compound still further the problems of translating the *Lao Tzu*, D. C. Lau argues that the work does not originate from one source but is really a collection of contributions, and that many of the chapters have disjointed additions that do not constitute a single, coherent theme.[13] At best, he contends, the *Lao Tzu* is an anthology; at worst it is a disjointed collection of fragments that are related only by a casual association of thoughts.

By all realistic accounts, a definitive English version of the *Lao Tzu* is made impossible by an overwhelming accumulation of obstacles. In Welch's words, "The Chinese classics are deep waters indeed, and I think we must recognize at the outset that of all of them, the [*Lao Tzu*] is the least susceptible to a definitive translation. We cannot be certain of what it means. We never will be."[14]

If the most fastidious and scholarly effort will not provide a definitive translation of the *Lao Tzu*, then there is room in the popular literature of Taoism for a carefully considered interpretation, particularly for one that expresses the old classic in a modern idiom.

THE QUESTION OF AUTHORSHIP

No definitive evidence supports the assumption that the *Lao Tzu* was written by a man of that name, although by about 225 B.C. tradition had assigned authorship to him. Indeed, there is no definitive evidence that Lao Tzu himself even existed.

Lao Tzu is a mystery. In a wonderfully Epimenidean paradox, he is reputed to have said, "As for the sage, no one will ever know whether he existed or not."[1] Even by 100 B.C. the Chinese historian Ssu-ma Ch'ien could not authenticate the existence of him.[2] Most subsequent scholarship on Lao Tzu is equally inconclusive; he is simply lost in the swirling mists of early Chinese history.

Because tradition has described such a person, history has attempted to substantiate him. One version, offered by Lin Yutang, has Lao Tzu born to a cultured family at K'uhsien in 571 B.C. In this version he eventually became Keeper of the Imperial Archives, was an older contemporary of

Confucius, and died at about 90 years of age.[3] Ssu-ma Ch'ien, however, has him living for 160 years.

Another version, cited by Holmes Welch, has Lao Tzu born on September 14, 604 B.C. in the kingdom of Ch'u. After being conceived by a falling star and spending 62 years in the womb, he arrived in this world as a silver-haired sage who promptly named himself and then proceeded to make profound philosophical pronouncements.[4] In 517 B.C. he allegedly ended his meetings with Confucius, who was 53 years his junior, by chastizing him for his foolishness. Then, at the age of 160, Lao Tzu departed into the West—a symbolic rejection of China—where a Buddhist source describes how he overcame the temptation of desire on three successive nights. A variation of this version has him born in Ch'en after being in the womb for 81 years—a propitious Buddhist number—and then departing into the West at age 200.

A less fanciful story identifies Lao Tzu as Lao Tan, an actual Keeper of the Imperial Archives about 374 B.C.[5] Had he been Lao Tan, however, he could not have had the reported conversations with Confucius, who by then would have been dead about a hundred years. Other speculation names Lao Tzu as Lao Lai Tzu or as Li Erh.

For a figure of such historical importance, Lao Tzu is suspiciously absent from the writings of the philosophers who immediately succeeded him. For example, according to the scholarship of D.C. Lau, the

Confucian Mencius (Meng-tse), who lived from about 371 B.C. to 289 B.C., does not indicate any awareness of Lao Tzu.[6] Even the writings attributed to Chuang Tzu and Lieh Tzu, the traditional successors of Lao Tzu, do not mention him. And their only reference to his writings is an occasional short quote which could easily have come from a traditional oral source.

There is simply no historical evidence that Lao Tzu ever existed. Perhaps a coalescing movement in Chinese thought personified itself in his character, and this image was then solidified and embellished by folklore, then used later by Taoists and even Buddhists to promote their particular interests. Arthur Waley suggests that in the common Chinese mind Lao Tzu may have become the composite of a number of ancient worthies.[7] If so, the solid image of a larger-than-life character as the author of an important corpus of literature could have become a habit too comfortable to abandon.

Curiously, this habit may have been encouraged by the Chinese language itself. Because Chinese contains neither definite nor indefinite articles, no recorded distinction could be made between references to Lao Tzu, the person, or to the *Lao Tzu*, the writings. Without this linguistic distinction, any mention of the writings could easily invent the notion of the person.

But other explanations could account for Lao Tzu's lack of definition in history. Authorship in ancient China is often difficult to substantiate because the Chinese of the day were vague about dates and authenticity. This may have been the result of casualness, but some scholarship suggests that it was deliberate, a tactic intended to confer venerable status—and thus credibility—on contemporary writings that otherwise would not be read.[8]

But a more respectable version of this explanation is offered by Waley.[9] Since the origin of writing in China was mnemonic—to record tradition so it would not be forgotten—the perfectly natural attitude would be to regard all writing as the preservation of tradition rather than the record of authorship. When authors of individual significance did appear, they were recorded with the same anonymity as earlier writers. No deception was intended. In the Chinese mind, there was no separate category for either living authors or dead ones because individual authorship did not formally exist. In the mind of the copyist, there was only traditional information; in the mind of the reader, there was no other kind of credible reading. Quite naturally, then, all knowledge was understood as traditional and only later came to be attributed to particular sources, to people who may or may not have existed. Such may have been the case with Lao Tzu.

The authenticity of the *Lao Tzu* did not become an issue to the Chinese, notes Waley, until they finally recognized individual authorship.[10] Then they had to confront the possibility that their most popular and signficant literary work might be something other than what it was commonly presumed to be. So the Chinese were forced to do one of two things: either discredit the work entirely and discard it from the canon of their literature, or allow a credibility to develop that would eventually authorize both the work and the author. So tradition came to accept and reinforce the notion that the *Lao Tzu* was the authentic creation of a single person. This acceptance was eventually so thoroughly integrated into the psyche of China that it became unchallenged history.

But Waley, despite the credibility of this argument, finished his scholarly 1958 translation of the *Lao Tzu* with the feeling that the work was the result of a single author because the conflicting elements were so subtly woven together "into a pattern perfectly harmonious and consistent."[11] Holmes Welch leaned toward the same position.[12] Alan Watts, who did not like the negative way in which modern textual criticism was applied to such issues of authorship, decided also that the consistency of content and style argued for one writer.[13] Then Waley apparently changed his mind as a result of persuasive argument from Fang Yu-lan, a fellow scholar who maintained that the Lao Tzu came from a variety of Taoist sources rather than a single author.[14] This position was also taken by D. C. Lau, who contended that the work is a fragmented collection of Taoist writings.[15] Textual criticism tends to endorse this contention. The recently discovered *Ma-wang-tui* texts nournish still further opinion.

With no solid evidence to support the existence of a Lao Tzu, his authenticity as a real historical character is extremely doubtful. The consequences of this doubt condenses into three questions. If there was no Lao Tzu, then who wrote the work attributed to him? If there was no author, then who collected, organized, and edited the source material into its existing form? And what are the implications if the *Lao Tzu* is simply a fragmented collection of Taoist material that lacks the coherent influence of a single mind?

All but the most fastidious scholars can dismiss the first question with relative ease. If the *Lao Tzu* was not written by Lao Tzu then it was written by someone else with a different name. That person is unknown, but for convenience can be called Lao Tzu.

Even the second question raises no serious concerns. If the Lao Tzu is a collection of Taoist wisdom, then someone did the collecting. A careful and insightful editorial process could deliberately transform a diverse body of wisdom into a focused, coherent, and cohesive philosophy. It is noteworthy that no proper names of sources or places appear in the *Lao Tzu*; either they were never present or they were meticulously deleted to give the collection a universal and timeless integrity. A sophisticated editorial process could be granted the equivalence of authorship. To add weight to this argument, chapters 20 and 70 of the traditional texts (chapters 64 and 35 in the *Ma-wang-tui* texts) are usually translated in the first person singular. The use of "I" suggests a particular person who steps out of the invisible role of the editor and into the personal voice of the writer. And chapter 42 (chapter 5 in the *Ma-wang-tui* texts) acknowledges that earlier teachings have been adopted; in other words, an "I" is employing the earlier wisdom of others.

But the third question makes translators and scholars uncomfortable. If the *Lao Tzu* is not the work of a single author or editor, then serious implications exist for both understanding and translating it into a consistent and unified work. Welch summarizes this concern by saying that it ". . . becomes not so much a puzzle as a hodgepodge."[16]

Many translators, however, are persuaded by their experience of the *Lao Tzu* that it is a unified whole. They find in it a consistency of style, mood, and personality that convinces them of its integrity as a single, literary entity by a single author or editor. Indeed, this seems to have been the experience of many readers for more than two thousand years.

If, in fact, the *Lao Tzu* really is a "hodgepodge," a disjointed collection of fragments, then what explains the experience of its integrity? The answer is that this quality is created solely in the minds of those who read it. The act of reading makes it whole. The fragments are knitted together by a diligence of thoughtful concentration and an ingenuity of creative consciousness such that a wholeness is made where there was none. So the *Lao Tzu* becomes a mirror in which all those who contemplate it are forced to view the wisdom inherent in themselves, a very Taoist metaphor for the meaning of meaning.

Just as each person must reach a private relationship with the utter perplexity of being, the individual reader must reach a private understanding with the Lao Tzu. The mystery of its totality is experienced by putting together what cannot rationally be put together, by following an integrative process that eludes explanation and description. Such an explanation also accounts for the undefineable nature of the Tao itself; it cannot be explained for the same reason that consciousness cannot explain itself. The clearest insights just are. They can be experienced only with the unconditional receptivity that happens in a whole and balanced presence with oneself.

The mandate of interpretation that has been assumed in *The New Lao Tzu* is wholly compatible with the notion that its essential source material is a disjointed collection of early Taoist writings. Such a condition not only replicates a proper approach to the Tao itself but it engenders the deepest kind of wisdom. No one can really understand either. Both the Tao and true wisdom are sensed as a nameless and amorphous order that underlies apparent disorder, are felt as a kind of formless insight that arises out of profound confusion.

Indeed, such an insight is accommodated when the *Lao Tzu* is a "hodgepodge" without the authenticity and authorship of a person called Lao Tzu.

THE
MA-WANG-TUI
TEXTS

At Ma-wang-tui, a village near Changsha in Hunan Province of central China, archeologists found, in the "Horse King Mound," two nearly complete silk texts of the *Lao Tzu*. An inventory slip confirms that the 1973 find was entombed on April 4th, 168 B.C. with the son of Li Ts'ang, a local nobleman and official.[1]

The *Ma-wang-tui* texts, some 500 years older than previous versions of the *Lao Tzu,* offer important insights into its origin and meaning. The scholarly study and subsequent translation of these texts has been used in the writing of *The New Lao Tzu.* Two translations are presently available, one by Robert G. Henricks and the other by Victor H. Mair. Henricks has translated the so-called Text B because it is more complete,[2] and Mair has translated Text A because it is older.[3] Manuscript disintegration has damaged both texts, but those portions missing in one are usually present in the other. The two texts are similar but not identical.

Henricks emphasizes that the *Ma-wang-tui* texts do not dramatically alter our reading of the *Lao Tzu* or our understanding of Taoist philosophy.[4] They are not revolutionary, and these recently found texts, therefore, do not render obsolete all previous translations and scholarship.

But the *Ma-wang-tui* texts are undoubtedly significant. They do question common assumptions about the origin of early Taoism, and they do differ in important details from the traditional texts, the ones that have been used as the basis for all previous translations of the *Lao Tzu*. And they do propose historical, philosophical, and scholarly challenges that will have to be confronted by anyone who is interested in a realistic and honest approach to Taoism.

The *Ma-wang-tui* texts are more grammatically precise than the traditional texts, notes Henricks,[5] so they can be more accurately translated. They have solved some of the word and phrase problems that have long bothered translators. And they have purged the *Lao Tzu* of some of the extraneous additions that have infiltrated it through centuries of copying, recopying, and editorializing. Consequently, a clearer sense of the early *Lao Tzu* is now available, one that suggests a less sectarian tradition that is more embracing in its philosophy and more universal in its spirituality than the traditional texts originally suggested. This combination of breadth and depth, incidentally, concurs with and rein-forces the perspective that initiated and guided the writing of *The New Lao Tzu.*

Of the detailed differences between the traditional versions of the *Lao Tzu* and the *Ma-wang-tui* texts, the most important is the arrangement of the so-called chapters.

Scholars have long considered that the *Lao Tzu* may have been made up of two separate sections, one addressing the subject of Tao and the other of Te. The *Ma-wang-tui* texts confirm this separation by actually labelling the two sections accordingly.[6] But it reverses their traditional order; the first section is called Te and the second Tao, so that chapters 1 through 37 now appear after chapters 38 through 81. The old classic, which has received its name from the order in which these two sections have appeared, may now have to be called the *Te Tao Ching* rather than the *Tao Te Ching.* Henricks acknowledges this change in the title of his book; Mair makes it in the subtitle of his, even suggesting in his preface that "the real title of this book should be something like *Sayings of the Old Masters.*"[7]

The *Ma-wang-tui* chapter order is different in other respects. The texts reverse chapters 40 and 41, put chapters 80 and 81 between 66 and 67, and place chapter 24 between chapters 21 and 22.

Significantly, the same order of chapters appears in both the Text A and the Text B versions of the *Ma-wang-tui* texts, confirming the validity of that order, and suggesting that the two different versions may have a common origin. The reversed halves also give some credibility to the notion that the *Lao Tzu* may have existed at one time as two separate books. Henricks does not consider the two-book theory but cites speculation that the two sections of the one book could have been ordered according to use. The Taoists who were concerned with matters of philosophy would have placed the Tao section first, and the so-called Legalists, who were concerned with matters of conduct, would have placed the Te section first.[8]

The rearranged chapter order in the *Lao Tzu* will undoubtedly provoke scholarly speculation. But the more immediate and tangible consequence will be a protracted controversy and some confusion about the naming, printing, and cataloging of a recognized classic that no longer has either an accepted title or an accepted order of contents. A resolution may take years to evolve as the habit of common usage interplays with the unfolding of authoritative opinion. Meanwhile, chapter order will continue to be a subject for the consideration of experts.

Henricks cites speculation that offers one possible explanation for the rearrangement of chapters. The *Ma-wang-tui* texts could have been copied from strips of bamboo, a bundle for Tao and another for Te. If the copyist misunderstood their order, or inadventently removed them in incorrect order, then the two sections would have been copied in reverse.[9] Any other rearrangement of the bamboo strips would account for the other changes in chapter order. If, however, Text A and Text B came from different sources—as it seems they did—yet have the same order of chapters, then this explanation seems unlikely. It is also unlikely that the bamboo strips were set out in chapters since these divisions occurred later. What, then, initiated the different order of chapters in the traditional texts? Perhaps it was some unknown version that appeared between the *Ma-wang-tui* texts and the traditional texts. But all this speculation presupposes that subsequent versions of the *Lao Tzu* came from one original text, a primary source. This may not be so.

What is known, however, is that the formidable task of translating from old Chinese to modern English still remains in the *Ma-wang-tui* texts. Mair, who has translated the older Text A, notes that it is "in many places maddeningly obscure and frustratingly ambiguous,"[10] and that sometimes he had to summon the muse of poetry to give poetic shape to his "rendition."[11] Henricks suggests on the dedication page of his book that his "interpretation" might generate some disagreement. He confesses that after the first draft of his translation was completed, he discussed with a friend "different ways in which the text might be read,"[12] and with a colleague he reviewed "a number of troubling passages."[13] Consequently, even when Henricks and Mair are both translating from Text A—as Henricks acknowledges he sometimes does when Text B is incomplete[14]—details in the same translated passages are different.

Organizing the *Ma-wang-tui* texts into stanzas and chapters still remains a problem. Like the earliest versions of the traditional texts, the *Ma-wang-tui* texts are nearly completely unbroken. "The text in each case essentially reads as one continuous whole," writes Henricks.[15] The two exceptions are the Te-Tao division—which is marked accordingly—and "in part II of Text A"[16] there are eighteen[17] "black dots between characters every so often (we might call them 'periods'), many of these but not all occurring at the beginning of present chapters."[18] If a translation of this text were to be literal and precise, it would yield a completely undivided Te section followed by a Tao section divided into nineteen chapters.

"It is futile," writes Mair, "to attempt to provide any rational basis for the division into eighty-one chapters since the number is purely arbitrary and has no organic bearing on the systematic ordering of the text."[19]

Henricks accounts for the number of chapters in Chinese terms. "The number eighty-one is a 'perfect' one in Yin/Yang speculations since nine is the fullness of Yang."[20] It follows that nine times nine is a greater fullness. Henricks thinks that eighty-one was probably settled upon by about 50 B.C.[21] This number of chapters, it is important to remember, is not derived from any textual source but has been imposed by later, exterior considerations.

Mair contends there is another basis for the eighty-one chapters; it is from Buddhism rather than Taoism. For Buddhists, as he points out, the number is "favored because it is the square of nine which was itself fraught with all manner of symbolic significance for Indian mystics. One of the most hallowed Buddhist scriptures, the *Prajnaparamita* sutra, also has eighty-one divisions."[22]

In addition to elaborating on a historical connection between Taoism and Buddhism, Mair takes the position, based on his analysis of the Ma-wang-tui texts, that the *Lao Tzu* evolved from a Chinese oral tradition which began as early as the seventh century B.C. and solidified into written form just before the end of the third century B.C.[23] He notes that the *Ma-wang-tui* texts show repetition and other mnemonic devices that characterize oral literature, and writing errors of the kind that are made during the conversion of the spoken word to the written one.[24] This would make the *Lao Tzu* a library of oral documents, a repository of memory that perhaps was first collected in written form in the *Ma-wang-tui* texts.

These writing errors deserve a little more attention because they provide a complicating twist to speculation about the early history of the *Lao Tzu*.

Some characters in the *Ma-wang-tui* texts have been deliberately blotted out, a clear indication that errors were made by the copyist. Such blotted out characters could have been made by a copyist who was careless but honest. Or they may have been made during dictation, as Mair suggests, by a copyist who was unsure of the correct written character as he tried to convert directly from the spoken language to its written form. There are eleven of these errors—a count is made possible by a facsimile representation in the back of Henricks's book. However, they occur only in Text B, the more recent of the *Ma-wang-tui* texts, not in the older Text A. Does this mean, in some curious reversal of the usual evolutionary process, that Text B came from an oral tradition of Taoism and Text A came from an earlier written tradition? Or were there two traditions, one oral and one written, that existed parallel to each other? If so, the history of the *Lao Tzu* prior to 168 B.C. is more complicated than the simple evolution of Taoist literature from an oral to a written form.

Any argument for an oral origin to Taoism casts further doubt upon the existence of Lao Tzu himself. Mair translates Lao Tzu simply as the Old Master, a name that, by inference, is more generic than specific. Such a name resonates with historical ambiguity and suggests that there may never have such a character. This position is somewhat substantiated by the inconclusive findings of Ssu-ma Ch'ien, the Chinese historian, who even in 100 B.C. was unable to substantiate the existence of Lao Tzu. And Mair writes, as if to confirm the nearly inevitable conclusion, "There is not a single shred of reliable biographical information concerning the identity of the Old Master."[25] This would apply whether the Old Master was author or editor.

If Mair is correct about an oral origin for the *Ma-wang-tui* texts, it means that the *Lao Tzu* is not the coherent and integrated work of an individual but a diverse collection of related wisdom held together by a common philosophy. Only the mnemonic and oral qualities of this tradition would explain its consistency of style. But the work could not be thought of or responded to as the effort of a single author. The implications are disturbing for anyone who wants to interpret it as the cohesive invention of one creative genius. If the *Lao Tzu* has a wholeness, it is either in the shared philosophy of its anonymous contributors or in the mind of each reader who experiences it as such.

Henricks contends that the *Ma-wang-tui* texts do not create a major shift in our reading of the *Lao Tzu*, that they primarily explain and correct certain detailed problems that have long puzzled translators.[26] This may be so.

But the discovery of these texts has changed dramatically the context in which this reading and understanding takes place. For those who use context to guide understanding, the *Ma-wang-tui* texts will be a catalyst for a significantly different perspective of the *Lao Tzu* and Taoism. The new experience will not necessarily be less, but it will be different because the background assumptions can no longer be the same. The recognition that the work is not likely the focused insight of a single mind should make it more challenging but less intimidating. It should offer a new freedom to those interested in Taoist philosophy and nudge the work farther from the folly of dogma; for those who are free-spirited enough to enjoy wandering the landscape of its words, there will be even fewer fences. And for the experts, the *Ma-wang-tui* texts will certainly invite productive speculation.

At present the existence of both a Text A and a Text B do confirm that different versions of the *Lao Tzu* were in circulation before 168 B.C. This is important historical information and it should fuel all manner of study and reappraisal by scholars.

For everyone else, the basic *Lao Tzu*—whether it is called the *Tao Te Ching* or the *Te Tao Ching*—remains intact, and more credible than ever. The *Ma-wang-tui* texts have shuffled its chapters, and its history has become less fictional. The misleading effects of two thousand years of inaccurate copying, deliberate editorializing, and questionable interpretation have themselves become history. Translation continues to be a challenge, although the latitude for wild options has been considerably reduced. Some layers of confusion have been peeled away and others have been revealed. But the old texts are again yielding new insights to an old wisdom. And the honest, searching inquiry they have already engendered is a welcome refreshment.

THE
CONTEMPORARY
INTERPRETATION

The translation process itself has made the *Lao Tzu* more difficult than it really is. The attempt of translators to be faithful to the literal meaning of the source material has scholarly merit, and has been of incomparable value to those in the West who have struggled with the elusive wisdom of the old classic. But translators have also preserved the cultural obscurities and eccentricities of ancient China that obstruct for modern readers their access to the essential wisdom of the *Lao Tzu*.

An interpretation of the *Lao Tzu* in the idiom of contemporary language and thought offers a different kind of faithfulness. As a translation of translations, it replaces a fidelity to literal detail with a sharper expression of the essential spirit of Taoism. By abandoning the Chinese mystique in favor of the working dynamics of Taoist philosophy, it reveals more clearly the simple and accessible wisdom that is at the heart of the *Lao Tzu*.

The New Lao Tzu, therefore, will seem less foreign and more familiar because it is not bound to the Chinese idiom; it does not attempt or purport to be faithful to a literal rendering of the Chinese texts. Every effort has been made to give the reader access to the essential wisdom of the original literature while expressing it in more friendly terms. Consequently, *The New Lao Tzu* should feel both authoritative and approachable.

The liberties that have been taken with the *Lao Tzu* texts range from minor to major, and have been guided by the express purpose of removing from the old classic its unnecessary difficulty while exposing its inherent wisdom. These liberties have been justified by the belief that this wisdom is essentially universal, and is wholly transferable from the time and place of its origin in China to current experience and practice in the modern West.

All changes are the result of reading the *Lao Tzu* less literally and more figuratively, of giving less attention to the words and more attention to their sense. Such a reading has made adjustments for the many historical and cultural differences that separate these civilizations by more than two thousand years.

This interpretation was the direct result of a careful examination of at least nine scholarly but very diverse translations of the *Lao Tzu*. These widely varied versions were chosen deliberately to give a broad base for approaching its wisdom; seven versions were from the traditional texts and two were from the recently discovered *Ma-wang-tui* texts. From these translations and other studies, the *Lao Tzu* was carefully transposed into the contemporary idiom.

Discerning and critical readers will hopefully appreciate that this option is not outlandish, considering that a literal rendering of the *Lao Tzu* is made virtually impossible by the gulfs of time, language, and culture that separate it from the present West. Access to its wisdom has always been compromised by translation difficulties and by text corruption in the Chinese sources. Indeed, a labyrinth of imprecision and uncertainty will invariably frustrate those who want a definitive English edition. No original text exists. No single Chinese version provides a definitive reference source. The translation problems are universally acknowledged to range from incredibly difficult to insurmountable. No evidence of an historical Lao Tzu offers the imprint of one mind to guide and focus the efforts of the translator, and the sheer absence of any evidence is building a conclusive case against the existence of any such individual. The Chinese scholar D. C. Lau, concludes that the *Lao Tzu* "is no more than a collection of passages with only a common tendency in thought."[1]

If the *Lao Tzu* was not created as a coherent whole by a single writer or editor, then its fragmented, disparate, and paradoxical threads can only be woven into a meaningful whole by those who read it. Alan Watts experienced the *Lao Tzu* as the coherent work of a single author.[2] Arthur Waley's first impression was that it had a unity and an integrity.[3] Since the variety of its themes must be integrated by some creative process, the worth of the *Lao Tzu* is not diminished if this activity takes place solely in the mind of the reader. Each reader, in a curious reversal of role, becomes author. "If you cannot get it from yourself," asks the Zen adage, "where will you go for it?"

The business of human consciousness is meaning. But meaning is not intrinsic in anything; it is made in minds. All experience is a disjointed tangle that must be organized and integrated into meaningful patterns by each thinking person. Indeed, as Victor H. Mair points out in his discussion of the *Ma-wang-tui* texts, the words thread, sew, stitch, suture, and sutra all have the same root.[4]

So each reader does with the *Lao Tzu* what each person must do with all experience—try to make sense of it. No one knows if the old classic is only a remotely connected collection of fragments, if it was created originally by a single author as a coherent whole, or if it evolved into such an integrated unit by a stringent editorial process; these are the fine points of historical dispute that will not be resolved at this time. The essential issue for the present is each reader's experience of the *Lao Tzu* as a provocative piece of insightful literature. In any form, it has always felt enticingly whole and meaningful. And it continues to feel so even if it is "a collection of passages with only a common tendency in thought." However uncertain its source or its integrity, this "common tendency" is enough. Unncertainty, when approached properly, is not a limiting deterrent but an inviting opportunity.

Indeed, uncertainty is always more interesting, more vital, more promising, and more enlivening than certainty. So in typically Taoist fashion, this obstacle of uncertainly that surrounds and permeates the *Lao Tzu* is transformed into productive possibility. It even becomes a metaphor for the elusive nature of the Tao itself.

So the very uncertainty of the *Lao Tzu* invites interpretation. The magic of mind is challenged to put together what may not be together, to stamp with cohesion a work that may not have such a unifying mark.

To call *The New Lao Tzu* an interpretation, therefore, is merely an outright declaration of the way the source material has always been treated, both officially and unofficially, by both translators and readers alike. No one knows exactly what it means. An interpretation simply assumes the freedom to untangle its threads and sew them together into a sutra. *The New Lao Tzu* is such a sewing, such a sutra. It is a tapestry offered to those who are willing to search its weave, feel its wholeness, and sense its wisdom. If this is marked with the mind of an interpreter, so be it.

For such an interpretation, a working text

was required. This text was derived from a careful word-by-word comparison of the nine source translations and then finding—as much as possible—their common ground. This was followed by creatively adjusting words and lines in the direction of clarity, integrity, and symmetry. Care was taken to retain the creative tension and balanced vitality between juxtaposing ideas and images.

Wherever possible *The New Lao Tzu* has been true to the words and images that were commonly agreed upon in the translations, provided they would be understood widely by modern readers.

When meaning was in doubt or inconsistencies appeared among translations, preference was given to the reading that concurred with the three cardinal principles in traditional philosophical Taoism: *tzu-jan, hsiang-sheng* and *wu-wei.*

Tzu-jan can be described approximately as spontaneity, the easy unfolding of circumstances that seem to occur when things are acting wholly in accord with their own natures. Inherent in the broadest understanding of *tzu-jan* is an implicit trust and respect for processes that are entirely natural, that concur with the ecology of the world's harmonious workings. More narrowly, *tzu-jan* trusts the spontaneity of individual action that arises when a sense of inner wholeness seems to be selflessly connected to outer wholeness. In this condition, individual volition seems to disappear, and the harmonious unfolding of events is experienced calmly and peacefully, without any sense of separation, tension, or willfulness.

Hsiang-sheng means mutual arising. It reflects the inseparable interconnectedness of all things, the inability of any single thing to be or act in isolation from the apparent opposites that define and interact with it. As a consequence of this principle, any untimely or untoward action that is not attuned to the natural unfolding of circumstances will evoke opposition and discord. The consequence of every self-centered act is resistance and the genesis of disorder. *Hsiang-sheng* assures that the balancing process within the equilibrium of wholeness is always functioning.

Wu-wei is a kind of non-doing. It is a mixture of both thoughtless volition and purposeful passivity, a kind of standing aside to let things do themselves. It is expressed positively as *wei-wu-wei,* doing without doing. When applied to individual volition, *wu-wei* has the effect of making an act spontaneous, a perfectly timed and appropriate reflex to the rightness of the moment.

Implicit in *tzu-jan, hsiang-sheng,* and *wu-wei* is an uneasiness about undue deliberation, about the compulsive, self-centered thinking that moves action away from its inherently human nature and, finally, away from Nature itself. Taoism, like Zen, is grounded in what is simply and profoundly natural.

Discerning readers will find in *The New Lao Tzu* a recognizable element of Zen. Indeed, the special psychological and philosophical forces that constitute one are also the essential qualities of the other. The development of Zen from Taoism can be traced through *Ch'an,* the Chinese amalgamation of Taoism and Buddhism that eventually migrated to Japan to become Zen Buddhism. The shape and mood of Zen is a little different from Taoism because of its historical evolution in the company of Buddhism and its context in Japan rather than China, but the Way of Zen and the Way of Tao can be understood to be synonymous.

The interpretive process that created *The New Lao Tzu* and associates itself with Zen, also dissociates itself from the *hsien* tradition of Taoism. *Hsien* literally means immortal or the immortals, and refers to those schools of Taoism that attempted by alchemic and yogic means to achieve immortality for their practitioners—some followers even pursued eternal life by seeking the proverbial fountain of youth on the elusive Isles of the Blest, P'eng-lai.[5] Because these schools appeared at least a hundred years after the recognized existence of the *Lao Tzu,* textual allusions to *hsien* accomplishments were either added by later transcribers or read into the Chinese by translators. In either case, the *hsien* tradition is not compatible with the philosophical one. Another very early yogic school of Taoism claimed its practitioners could walk on water without sinking or in fire without being burned, could levitate, and could have boundless longevity.[6] This, too, is a variation of *hsien* and does not have a place in this interpretation of the *Lao Tzu*.

The New Lao Tzu has assiduously avoided any suggestion of superstition and metaphysics. It does not attribute to the sage any kind of supernatural powers. Ultimately, the sage is ordinary, a person bounded by the same natural limitations as everyone. No sagely powers can slough off the skin of old age so the body can emerge reborn and renewed. Like everyone, the sage eventually dies. Like everyone, the sage can be helpful to the world only by moving in accordance with its principles. No supernatural powers are at play in the sage's art, and none are implied in this interpretation.

The sage can only master the world by becoming one with it. No magic, nothing extraordinary is involved. Skills are earned by reflection, by insight, and by cultivated intuition; then they are honed by a deep empathy that attunes to the inherent nature of the world itself. Experience occupies the place of belief. Philosophical Taoism, therefore, is not sensational, not spectacular. When practiced best, it is so unobtrusive and inconspicuous that it is hardly even noticed.

Such a quality reverberates so clearly throughout the *Lao Tzu* that the precise and assertive character of English is an inherently awkward medium for it. This language is an idiom of thought and expression that has a shortage of words with the appropriate connotative neutrality. Words are needed that have enough passivity to suggest the softness of Taoism, yet have enough weight to convey the strength of this softness. Since a language like English is the expression of a deliberate and volitional culture, its words have difficulty suggesting the subtlety and quietly accommodating balance of Taoist philosophy.

Words move through history and undergo connotative shifts; similar shifts occur when they are moved by translation from one culture to another. Since both shifts apply to any English version of the *Lao Tzu*, particular care had to be taken with the modern words that were offered by the literal translations of the Chinese texts. If their connotations had shifted enough that they were no longer compatible with a contemporary understanding of Taoist philosophy, they were changed.

Some ancient Chinese cultural allusions also had to be changed because they would not transpose into the modern West and retain the metaphorical meaning that was originally intended. Other passages in *The New Lao Tzu* were moderated if the direct translation of the Chinese jeopardized understanding or credibility because the style was too exaggerated, overly florid, or excessively metaphorical.

A distinction was made between those parts of the *Lao Tzu* that seem to be universal and timeless, and those parts that no longer reflect accepted realities. In the latter case, such parts were adjusted or excluded. Accordingly, some changes were made to concur with the political and psychological realities of today; that power, for example, is granted to leaders, not assumed by rulers.

Other minor changes were made. The masculine gender bias of the translations was eliminated. And the traditional use of the "I" in the three previously mentioned chapters was changed to favor a consistent voice.

Some specific images were focused more sharply in *The New Lao Tzu* to highlight their importance in the source material. Other ideas that were implicit in certain passages but not explicitly stated were added in the interpretation to enlarge and clarify the intended meaning. In contrast, other passages were deliberately left sparse when this austerity of words served the deeper purpose of suggesting rather than stating, of pointing rather than explaining.

The sense of grounded practicality that pervades the *Lao Tzu* has been kept. The worldly observations and advice that come from it have the clear objective of effecting balance and harmony through the wisdom of each individual's spontaneous action or inaction.

The traditional eighty-one chapters of the *Lao Tzu* have been kept. Nothing was moved from one chapter to another. Sometimes the stanza divisions were adjusted slightly so that different thoughts could be appropriately separated, juxtaposed, or related. But the stanza divisions in *The New Lao Tzu* remain fairly orthodox, even though translators only vaguely agree where they should be.

In keeping with tradition, each chapter of the *Lao Tzu* was considered to be a single, unified theme, although some chapters are clearly extensions of previous ones. It is worth remembering that the oldest Chinese texts have few chapter divisions; one flows into the next as a nearly continuous whole.

Although more than half the historic *Lao Tzu* texts are rhymed in their Chinese form, *The New Lao Tzu* has deliberately avoided the stilted and constrained effects of imposing such a style. Priority has been given to the clear and easy expression of insights, advice, and wisdom. The free verse that is used is without stylistic artifice, and might almost be mistaken for prose.

In some chapters the order of lines in the *Lao Tzu* was adjusted so the sequence of thought felt more logical. Other ideas that were expressed subtly in the source translations were deliberately amplified so their connection with adjacent ideas would be more apparent. To accommodate the West's more linear style of thinking, intermediate lines were sometimes added as intellectual bridges so the conceptual distance between one thought and the next was not so great.

But other changes are more significant. Modern readers in the West should not be surprised to discover that a text coming from a very different culture of more than two thousand years ago express- es itself in a style that does not correspond to our own. Certain passages of the *Lao Tzu*, when translated too literally, are uncomfortably convoluted and obtuse. These passages required considerable rewriting.

Fundamental attitudes have also changed. A modern society that is information and knowledge saturated will have difficulty reconciling itself with the *Lao Tzu's* pronouncements that learning is the source of trouble, and that people are appropriately managed by keeping them ignorant and simple. Clearly, this attitude and strategy cannot be applied in the present age. The two positions, however, can be reconciled. It is possible to be extremely sophisticated yet remain fundamentally simple and grounded. This is, after all, the traditional quality of the sage, a person who recognizes with uncomplicated clarity the earthy wisdom that binds everyone and everything to the inevitable rhythms of a natural life. No amount of sophistication has ever transported anyone beyond the limiting bounds of ordinary humanity. So *The New Lao Tzu* condones learning, but recognizes that it has to be grounded and balanced by profound simplicity. This philosophical adjustment required careful rewriting of the source material.

Finally, reordering the chapters, including

reversing the so-called Tao and Te sections, was perhaps the most obvious change that had to be made to the *Lao Tzu*. This change was made reluctantly because tradition deserves respect. But the authority of the recently discovered *Ma-wang-tui* texts seems unquestionable, and these silken artifacts are presently the most reliable indication of the original form of the old classic. Therefore the chapters in *The New Lao Tzu* are ordered according to these texts.

This change in chapter order has now created the contentious issue of whether the old classic should be called the *Tao Te Ching* or the *Te Tao Ching*. Popular usage may eventually resolve the matter. But some perspective is offered by the reminder that its traditional name has been assumed by a later usage that accepted the order and placement of its two principal sections into one volume. It was probably first known to the Chinese as simply *Lao Tzu*, literally Old Master, a title that was undefined by either a definite or indefinite article, and alluded to neither the number nor the order of its sections. *The New Lao Tzu*, therefore, revives the original tradition. This has been done to avoid the sectional problem but, more importantly, to remind the reader that however ancient the source, it is viable only if it remains both old and new; the root must continue to nourish a wisdom that is fresh and living.

The ancient Way must be lived in the moving instant of the present. While the historical Tao is the domain of the scholar, the real Tao exists only in the passing dynamics of each unfolding moment. For those who wish to follow its elusive Way, to move with its moving, to ride in balance upon the crest of its becoming and being, perhaps the old wisdom will be more apparent if it is expressed in new words.

SOURCES
AND
INDEX

THE SOURCE
TRANSLATIONS

Feng, Gia-Fu and English, Jane. *Lao Tzu: Tao Te Ching*. New York: Vintage Books, 1972.

Henricks, Robert G. *Lao-Tzu: Te-Tao Ching: A New Translation Based on the Recently Discovered Ma-wang-tui Texts*. New York: Ballantine, 1989.

Lau, D.C. *Lao Tzu: Tao Te Ching*. Hammondsworth, England: Penguin Books, 1963.

Maurer, Herrymon. *Tao: The Way of the Ways*. Aldershot, Great Britain: Wildwood House, 1982.

Mair, Victor H. *Tao Te Ching: The Classic Book of Integrity and the Way*. New York: Bantam Books, 1990.

Yutang, Lin. *The Wisdom of Laotse*. New York, The Modern Library (Random House), 1948.

Waley, Arthur. *The Way and its Power: A Study of the Tao Te Ching and Its Place in Chinese Thought*. New York: Grove Press, 1958.

Wing, R. L. *The Tao of Power: A Translation of the Tao Te Ching by Lao Tzu.* New York: A Dolphin Book/ Doubleday, 1986.

Wu, John C. H. *Lao Tzu/Tao Teh Ching.* New York: St. John's University Press, 1961.

NOTES

THE TRANSLATION PROBLEM

1. Holmes Welch, *Taoism: The Parting of the Way* (Boston: Beacon Press, 1957), p. 4.
2. Ibid., p. 12.
3. Arthur Waley, *The Way and Its Power: A Study of the Tao Te Ching and Its Place in Chinese Thought* (New York: Grove Press, 1958), p. 61.
4. Ibid., p. 62.
5. Welch, op. cit., pp. 9-11.
6. Ibid., p. 12.
7. Victor H. Mair, trans. *Tao Te Ching: The Classic Book of Integrity and the Way* (New York: Bantam, 1990), p. 131.
8. John C.H. Wu, trans. *Lao Tzu: Tao Teh Ching* (New York: St. John's University Press, 1961), pp. ix-x.
9. Robert G. Henricks, trans. *Lao-Tzu: Te-Tao Ching* (New York: Ballantine Books, 1989), p. xiv.
10. Ibid., p. xiv.
11. Waley, op. cit., p. 128.

12. Mair, op. cit., p. 152.

13. D. C. Lau, trans. *Lao Tzu: Tao Te Ching* (New York: Penguin Books, 1963), p. 165.

14. Welch, op. cit., p. 13.

THE QUESTION OF AUTHORSHIP

1. Holmes Welch, *Taoism: The Parting of the Way* (Boston: Beacon Press, 1957), p. 1.

2. Arthur Waley, *The Way and Its Power: A Study of the Tao Te Ching and Its Place in Chinese Thought* (New York: Grove Press, 1958), p. 106.

3. Lin Yutang, *The Wisdom of Laotse* (New York: The Modern Library, 1948), p. 8.

4. Welch, op. cit., p. 2.

5. Waley, op. cit., p. 104.

6. D. C. Lau, trans. *Lao Tzu: Tao Te Ching* (New York: Penguin Books, 1963), p. 158.

7. Welch, op. cit., p. 3.

8. Ibid., p. 3.

9. Waley, op. cit., pp. 102-3.

10. Ibid., p. 105.

11. Ibid., p. 97.

12. Welch, op. cit., p. 179.

13. Alan Watts, *Tao: The Watercourse Way* (New York: Pantheon Books, 1975), p. xxiii.

14. Welch, op. cit., p. 179.

15. Lau, op. cit., p. 165.

16. Welch, op. cit., p. 179.

THE MA-WANG-TUI TEXTS

1. Robert G. Henricks, trans. *Lao-Tzu: Te-Tao Ching* (New York: Ballantine Books, 1989), p. xii.
2. Ibid., p. 3.
3. Victor H. Mair, trans. *Tao Te Ching: The Classic Book of Integrity and the Way* (New York: Bantam, 1990), p. 151.
4. Henricks, op. cit., p. xv.
5. Ibid., p. xvi.
6. Ibid., p. xiv.
7. Mair, op. cit., p. xv.
8. Henricks, op. cit., pp. xvi-xvii.
9. Ibid., p. xvii.
10. Mair, op. cit., p. xiv.
11. Ibid., p. xiv.
12. Henricks, op. cit., p. ix.
13. Ibid., p. ix.
14. Ibid., p. 3.
15. Ibid., p. xvii.
16. Ibid., p. xvii.
17. Ibid., p. 264.
18. Ibid., p. xvii.
19. Mair, op. cit., p. 152.
20. Henricks, op. cit., p. xvii.
21. Ibid., p. xvii.
22. Mair, op. cit., p. 152.
23. Ibid., pp. 119-20, 123.
24. Ibid., p. 121.

25. Ibid., p. 119.

26. Henricks, op. cit., p. xv.

THE CONTEMPORARY INTERPRETATION

1. D. C. Lau, trans. *Lao Tzu: Tao Te Ching* (New
York: Penguin Books, 1963), p. 165.

2. Alan Watts, *Tao: The Watercourse Way* (New York:
Pantheon Books, 1975), p. xxiv.

3. Arthur Waley, *The Way and Its Power: A Study of the
Tao Te Ching and Its Place in Chinese Thought*
(New York: Grove Press, 1958), p. 97.

4. Victor H. Mair, trans. *Tao Te Ching: The Classic
Book of Integrity and the Way* (New York:
Bantam, 1990), p. 136.

5. Holmes Welch, *Taoism: The Parting of the Way*
(Boston: Beacon Press, 1957), p. 97.

6. Mair, op. cit., pp. 146-47.

BIBLIOGRAPHY

Campbell, Joseph. *Myths To Live By.* New York:
Bantam Books, 1973.

Campbell, Joseph (with Bill Moyers). *The Power Of
Myth.* New York: Doubleday, 1988.

Capra, Fritjof. *The Tao Of Physics: An Exploration of
the Parallels Between Modern Physics and Eastern
Mysticism.* Berkeley: Shambhala, 1975.

Cavendish, Richard. *The Great Religions.* London:
Contact, 1980.

Hayward, Jeremy W. *Shifting Worlds, Changing
Minds: Where the Sciences and Buddhism Meet.*
Boston: Shambhala, 1987.

Hofstadter, Douglas R. Godel, *Escher, Bach: An
Eternal Golden Braid.* New York: Vintage
Books, 1979.

Koestler, Arthur. *The Roots of Coincidence.* New York:
Vintage Books (Random House), 1973.

Kraft, Kenneth, ed. Zen: *Tradition and Transition.*
New York: Grove Press, 1988.

Maurer, Herrymon. *Tao: The Way of The Ways.*
Aldershot, England: Wildwood House, 1986.

Moore, Charles R., ed. *The Chinese Mind: Essentials of
Chinese Philosophy and Culture.* Honolulu: The
University Press of Hawaii, 1967.

Morris, Ivan, ed. *Madly Singing in the Mountains: An
Appreciation and Anthology of Arthur Waley.*
Berkeley: Creative Arts Book Company, 1981.

Phen, S. T. *Three Character Classic.* Singapore: EPB
Publishers, 1989.

Watts, Alan. *Tao: The Watercourse Way.* New York:
Pantheon Books, 1975.

Welch, Holmes. *Taoism: The Parting of the Way.*
Boston: Beacon Press, 1965.

INDEX OF
SUBJECTS

Defending: and wisdom, 41

Deprivation: and armies, 99; and the use of force, 99

Desire: and being, 53; creates discontent, 63; and a peaceful end, 12; and those who master, 12; the greatest misfortune, 14; and the sage, 36; and the ancient sages, 78; and nameless simplicity, 107; and the Tao, 60; tempering, 83

Desire, without: and the Tao, 60

Destroyed: the formless cannot be, 68

Destruction: and weapons, 100

Details: attending to, 69

Devastation: and armies, 99; and the use of force, 99

Die: the not born does not, 68

Difficult: and easy, 61

Difficult, the: and attending to while easy, 35

Differences: and shifting balance, 9; defining each other, 9; and explaining each other, 9; and harmony, 9

Direction: trust and inner, 35

Disapproval: and approval, 84

Disaster: as the source of heroes, 82; and avoided by the path of life, 18

Discipline, inner: see Inner discipline

Disciplined, the: are favored, 49

Discontent: the greatest curse, 14; and desire, 63

Discord: and remembered grievances, 56; and propriety, 2

Disgrace: as the condition of self, 74

Dishonest, the: and nourishing trust, 17

Disorder: and disturbing order, 31

Does: without doing, 15

Doing: the best does itself, 11, 81; without doing, 61; without expecting, 53; and failing, 36; and grace, 36; doing itself, 36; without recognition, 61; and resistance, 99; the sage and best, 11; things doing themselves, 16; the proper things, 84

Door: without stepping beyond, 15

Dying: and the nourishing female, 71; when not different from living, 71

Earth, the: the sage living close to, 55; and oneness, 4; and stillness, 4

Easy: and difficult, 61; and the ancient sages, 78

Easy, the: before it becomes difficult, 35

Flavors: overcome the keenness of tasting, 73

Followers: and order, 4

Following: consists of emptying, 16; mastering people by, 27; the ancient path by emptying, 26; the Way, 36; the effortless way, 35; the Great Mother's wisdom

Fool, the: and the sage, 46; do not know they do not know, 47

Foolish, the: when they hear of the Tao, 6

Foolishness: recognizing, 47

Footprints: and the best walking, 95

Force: and ease with the world, 103; and exhaustion, 91; and the beginning of failure, 99; and fear, 48; and mastering others, 103; and people, 48, 91; and the creation of resistance, 99; and the right-hand of, 100; and the sage, 48, 91; and the Tao, 99; and following the Tao, 91

Forgetting: ideas, 26; words, 26

Form: and emptiness, 66; as body of the Great Mother, 20; and the formless, 11, 89; the formless as eternal, 6

Formless, the: and comfort, 105; and endurance, 105; cannot be destroyed, 68; and form, 89; as eternal form, 6; greater than form, 11; and fulfillment, 105; and order, 86; and peace, 105; returning to, 83

Front: and back, 61

Fulfillment: and death, 103; and the formless, 105; of a great nation, 32; of a small nation, 32; and people, 95; and the sage, 89; by being selfless, 68

Fulfilling: the world as, 20

Fullness: and emptiness, 89; is empty, 13

Funerals: and victory, 100

Gaining: and losing, 61, 89; is followed by losing, 106

Generosity: of the mystery, 67; of the Great Mother, 19

Gentleness: and the left-hand of, 100; and the sage, 100

Getting: usefulness of, 12

Glory: and victory, 99

Giving: and being enriched, 41

Good: and bad, 29; creates bad, 61; water is like the highest, 69

Good, the: and acceptance of, 17; are rewarded by the Tao, 33

Governing: a large country, 31; and the Tao, 31

Government: offerings to, 33; installation of, 33

Grace: arising from no burdens, 36; and the sage, 41

Great Mother, the: as the beginning, 20; the body of everything, 19; as form, 20; and fullness, 67; generosity of, 19; and the living mystery, 97; as mystery, 60; the mystery of, 67; and the nature of the world, 97; in serving, 30; as substance, 20; and the Tao, 19, 20, 60; vitality of, 19; wisdom of, 20; and wisdom, 30; and the wisdom of the dark, 97; as the world, 20

Greatness: and humility, 89; and the ordinary, 104; and the Tao, 104

Greed: the greatest burden, 14

Grievances: and peace, 56

Guiding: by giving no direction, 95

Hard: as the way of the dying, 52

Hardness: becomes the same as softness, 71; overcome by softness, 11; overcome by softness and weakness, 106

Harmonious accord: and primal simplicity, 97

Harmony: and shifting balance, 9; cultivating before discord arises, 36; the simple as the guardians of, 38; of oneness, 61; and opposites, 9; and rhythms, 61; and softening, 80; and wholeness, 71

Having: without possessing, 53

Hearing: dulled by loud sounds, 73; and the Tao; 76

Heaviness: and lightness, 94

Herding: and rituals, 84

Heroes: appear from disasters, 82

Hidden: the sage relies on the, 48

High: and low, 61

Highest, the: and the lowest, 97; the perfection of, 97

Honest: with others be, 69

Honest, the: and trust of, 17

Honor: and boasting, 88; and disgrace, 70; and dying, 74; and entrusted with the world, 74

Humble, the: will overcome, 52

Humility: tempers ambition, 63; and people in small countries, 40; and greatness, 89; and influence, 42; and the sage, 39; embraced by the sage, 55; and strength, 44; one of three treasures, 42; and understanding, 4

Hurrying: and sustaining a pace, 88

Hypocrisy: and ingenuity, 82

Ideas: forgetting of, 26

Ignorance: recognizing the ignorance in, 47

Impartiality: and the sage, 66; and the Tao, 56; and those who follow the
    Tao, 56; and the universe, 66

Imperfect, the: as perfection, 13; and vitality, 13

Impossible, the: composed of the possible, 35

Improper: and proper, 84

Increasing: followed by decreasing, 106

Infants, newborn: and undivided attention, 24; unaware of differences,
    24; and the primal source, 24; and inner stillness, 24; and strength,
    24; and the Tao, 24

Influence: and humility, 42

Ingenuity: abandoning of, 26; and knowledge, 82; and swindlers, 83; and
    thieves, 83

Injury: avoided by the path of life, 18

Inner: moving as one with outer, 71; the sage trusts the, 48

Inner balance: and the opposites of the world, 98; and the sage, 66, 98;
    and stillness, 66; and a greater wisdom, 98

Inner discipline: is favored by the world, 35

Inside: the sage is guided by what is, 73

Insight: and acceptance, 24; and the deepest constant, 24; and the
    senses, 73; and simplicity, 42

Intangible, the: and substance, 86

Integrity: and fulfillment, 19; and the Tao, 19; value of, 12

Intent: the ancient sages seem to be, 78

Is: as guidance to sage, 2; and what can be known, 86; world is known
    by, 8; made useful by what is not, 72

Is not: is known by, 8

Jewel: honored by sage, 4

Joy: and creatures, 4; and victory, 100

Just: with others be, 69

Justice: governing a country with, 27; and the Tao, 2

Killing: and the celebration of victory, 100

Kindness: and the Tao, 2

Knots: the best cannot be untied, 95

Knowing: and explaining, 26; the Tao, 107

Knowledge: and propriety, 82; and virtue, 82

Knows: without understanding, 15

Land: live close to the, 69

Last: and first, 68

Laughter: when the foolish hear of the Tao, 6

Law: and poverty, 27; and the Tao, 1/38

Leaders: and accomplishments, 81; and action in a crisis, 94; and contentment, 29; and control by, 29; everyone thinks, 81; and excess,
21; feared, 81; loved, 81; and luxury, 21; the best are hardly noticed,
81; and order, 4; the best are never reckless, 44; ridiculed, 81; as
common thieves, 21; and trust, 81

Leadership: those who can be entrusted with, 74

Leading: by following, 95; people, 30

Learning: consists of filling, 16

Least, the: becoming the greatest, 55; closest to most, 30; and primal
virtue, 30

Left-hand, the: and gentleness, 100

Less: is better than more, 30

Life: born into, 18; and dying, 74; and honor, 74; and misfortune, 74; at
one with, 18; the path of, 18; value too lightly, 18; waste of, 18; and
wealth, 74

Light, the: know the brightness of, 97; and the dark, 97; and the Great
Mother, 97; and the living mystery, 97

Lightness: and heaviness, 94; from the root of heaviness, 94

Limits, natural: see Natural limits

Living: when not different from dying, 71; and the nourishing female, 71

Living mystery, the: and the wisdom of the dark, 97

Living stream, the: and the humility of the lowest, 97; and the deepest
places, 97; and primal simplicity, 97

Living valley, the: and the feminine, 97; and the primal beginning, 97;
and the Tao, 97

Locks: the best cannot be opened, 95

Long: and short, 61

Loser: unwise to provoke the, 56

Losing: as a way of finding, 9; and gaining, 61, 106; to gain, 89;

New: and old, 98; and the ways of the world, 98

Non-being: and being, 61

Nothing: receiving the bounty of the world by claiming, 89

Nourishing: and acceptance, 17; and trust, 17

Nourishment: and primal simplicity, 97; and the Tao, 105; and valleys, 4

Obligation: and virtue, 2

Oceans: are below rivers, 39

Old: and new, 98; and the ways of the world, 98

Oneness: not disturbed, 61; and earth, 4; everything moves in, 4; cannot
    be explained, 9; and grace of, 61; and harmony, 61; and people, 95;
    and the sage, 95; and sky, 4; and the Tao, 9, 60; and teaching, 95;
    and twoness, 9; and valleys, 4; and wisdom, 4, 95; and wisdom of,
    95; and wonder, 60; with the world, 91

Opening: and opportunities, 30; and the Way, 36; and following the
    Great Mother's wisdom, 30

Opportunities: and primal virtue, 30

Opposites: and shifting balance, 9; the sage balances, 13; chasing in cir-
    cles, 29; defining each other, 9; and explaining each other, 9; and
    harmony, 9; and inner balance, 98; and the sage, 98; and a greater
    wisdom, 98; of the world, 98

Opposition: provoked by, 39; provoked by power that is apparent, 2

Order: and contentment of people, 63; when nothing disturbs, 31;
    and followers, 4; from the formless, 65/2; maintains itself, 48; and
    leaders, 4; no one sees the, 46; and oneness, 61, 95; and rhythms
    natural, 61, 101; and no struggle, 69; and the Tao, 101; the world
    has an, 46

Order, natural: see Natural order

Ordinary: and greatness, 104; the Tao as, 63; 104; 105

Ordinary, the: and the Tao, 63; when they hear of the Tao, 6; as greatest
    gift, 33; as the highest virtue, 6

Others: and mastering with force, 103; and understanding, 103

Outer: moving as one with inner, 71

Overcoming: by yielding, 89

Pace: hurrying and sustaining a, 88

Parts: and names, 101; and thinking, 101; and wholeness, 101

Path: easiest is the most difficult to follow, 6

Path, of life: avoiding danger 18; avoiding disaster, 18; untouched by threat, 18; untouched by injury, 18; and weapons, 18

Path, the: finding by leaving hidden, 29; following by emptying, 26

Peace: and the formless, 105; and forgetting grievances, 56; honored,
100; of simple people, 51

Peaceful: and the ancient sages amid turmoil, 78;

People: affairs of as one of four great powers, 92; and the bad, 95; at
birth, 52; and contentment, 63, 95; and control of themselves, 95; in
large countries, 40; in small countries, 40; at death, 52; and not
afraid of death, 51; threatened with death, 50; without desire, 107;
eagerly doing the proper things, 84; and fulfillment, 95; and the
good, 95; and hunger, 51; and nameless simplicity, 107; and oneness, 95; and the natural order, 107; and order, 95; and peaceful
order, 63; and respect, 95; and restlessness, 51; and the sage receiving, 17; and their natural selves, 83; strive upward, 69; and fulfilling
themselves, 27; governing themselves, 27; and poverty, 51; and
prosperity of, 27; and struggle, 63; as uncomplicated, 40; unlike
water, 69; and the workings of the world, 92

Perfect, the: is imperfect, 6

Perfection: is imperfect, 13

Plants: when alive, 52; when dead, 52

Possessing: and having, 53; and losing, 36; and loss, 12; and the sage, 36;
the world, 98; and losing the world, 98

Possible, the: and the impossible, 35

Poverty: and control, 27; and laws, 27; and regulations, 27; and restlessness, 27

Power: that is apparent, 2; and the display of, 106; that provokes opposition, 2; and no power, 44; and pride, 44; that cannot be resisted, 2;
that is unnoticed, 2; greatest is unnoticed, 6; and virtue as one, 86

Power, the greatest: does not control, 19; does not influence, 19; does not
interfere, 19

Powers: the four great, 92

Praise: creates rivalry, 63

Pretention: and virtue, 2

Pride: and dying, 74; and being entrusted with leadership, 74; and
power, 44; and success, 99; and understanding, 88

Primal beginning, the: and the feminine, 97; and the living valley, 97;
and the masculine, 97; and the Tao, 97

River: and the sea, 101; below streams, 39; and the valley stream, 101; and following the Tao, 101

Room: useful because of its emptiness, 72

Roots: deep in solid ground, 30; and lasting results, 30

Ruthless: the world as, 20

Saints: the benefit of being without, 83

Sage, the: and accord, 63; ahead by being behind, 68; arriving without leaving, 15; and balance, 66; returns to the natural balance, 53; keeps to the beginning, 15; stays behind, 39; stays below, 39; benefit of being without, 83; welcomes bitterness, 55; and no burdens, 36; and no desire, 36; is without desire, 27; and difficulty, 35; does without doing, 11, 15, 61; doing less and less, 16; does nothing, 27, 36, 48; lives close to the earth, 55; and endings, 70; finds without seeking, 15; and gentleness, 100; guided by deep, 2; guides by giving no directions, 95; empties, 41; balancing extremes, 63; and the wheel's hub, 72; and inner balance, 98; is mistaken for the fool, 46; and foolishness, 47; and force, 48; and the use of force, 91; and fulfillment, 89; and grace, 41; and the hidden, 48; and humility, 39; embraces humility, 55; and ignorance, 47; and impartiality, 66; and the inner, 48; guided by what is inside, 73; does not interfere, 27; guided by what is, 2; guided by the unknown, 2; and the jewel, 4; knows without understanding, 15; leads by following, 95; does not lead, 39; and being lost, 9; does not measure, 4; possesses nothing, 36; does not oppose, 39; and opposites, 98; balances opposites, 13; becoming one with the world, 89; and order, 48; as ordinary, 38; provokes no one, 27; does not resist, 39; and selflessness, 17; and inner sense, 2; and separateness, 9; and the wisdom of simplicity, 38; and the strength of softness, 42; and stillness, 66; moving with an inner stillness, 13; and stone, 4; does not struggle, 89; guided by the subtle, 73; chooses the Tao, 29; honors the Tao, 55; and thoughtlessness, 17; teaches without words, 11; and the feeling of being unworthy, 9; and weapons, 100; and a greater wisdom, 98; and the wisdom of oneness, 95; works without effort, 11; follows by yielding, 8

Sages, the ancient: see Ancient sages

Sea: and the river, 101; and following the Tao, 101; and the valley stream, 101

Seeing: blinded by bright colors, 73; and the Tao, 76

Seeking: and the Tao, 33

Seers: and trouble, 2

Self: abandoning, 83; and disgrace, 74; and pride, 74; and strength, 103; unimportance of, 74; and vanity, 74; and wisdom, 103

Selflessness: and being fulfilled, 68; and the sage, 17

Separate: and the sage's feeling of being, 9

Serenity: as treasure, 103

Shape: largest is boundless, 6

Shifting balance: and harmony, 9; and opposites, 9

Short: and long, 61

Show, outer: and sage, 2

Silence: and sound, 61; as the finest sound, 6

Simplicity: honor of, 83; and insight, 42; and primal virtue, 2; one of three treasures, 42; and understanding, 63; the wisdom of, 38

Simplicity, nameless: see Nameless simplicity

Simplicity, primal: see Primal simplicity

Sky: and oneness, 4; and vision, 4

Soft: as the way of the living, 52

Softening: and timeless balance, 80; and timeless harmony, 80; and the inside self, 80; and the Tao, 80; and tranquility, 80

Softness: and compassion, 42; becomes the same as hardness, 71; overcomes hardness, 11; and overcoming hardness, 106; and the sage, 42; and strength, 42; and overcoming strength, 106; of water, 55

Solid: and the ancient sages, 78

Sound: and the sharpness of hearing, 73; and silence, 61; the finest is silence, 6

Source: as generosity, 67; as mystery, 67

Source, dark: of the Great Mother, 60; of the Tao, 60

Source, primal: see Primal source

Standing: and balance, 88; on tiptoe, 88

Still: and moving, 98; and the ways of the world, 98

Stillness: and action, 94; and earth, 4; and emptiness, 80; of the female overcomes the male, 32; and newborn infants, 24; the sage moving with an inner, 13

Stillness, peaceful: and balance, 66; and the sage, 66

Stone: honored by sage, 4

Stopping: and avoiding trouble, 101; and dividing wholeness, 101

Straight: bending and remaining, 89

Stream: see Valley stream

Stream, living: see Living stream

Streams: and rivers, 39

Strength: and compassion, 42; restrained by compassion, 63; and the
  enduring center, 103; and humility, 44; as inflexible, 52; and mastering self, 103; and softness, 42; overcome by softness, 106; overcome
  by weakness, 106

Strengthening: followed by weakening, 106

Strong: and weak, 98; and the ways of the world, 98

Struggle: and accomplishments, 91; and exhaustion, 91; the natural
  order and no, 69; and resistance, 89

Substance: as the body of the Great Mother, 20; and the intangible, 86

Subtle: the sage is guided by the, 73

Subtlety: and the Tao, 76

Success: and pride, 99

Summer: be still in the heat of, 13

Suspicion: and propriety, 2

Swindlers: and ingenuity, 83; and profit, 83

Systems: and thinking, 101; and divided wholeness, 101

Tactics: of war, 45

Tao, the: all things move in accord with, 33; cannot be avoided, 26; and
  the beginning, 60; as the beginning of the beginning, 65; as no
  beginning, 76; and unnecessary behaviors, 88; like the bending of a
  bow, 53; and ceremony, 2; and compassion, 2; as a constant, 76; and
  control, 104; does not control, 19; its course is precise and unerring,
  49; as dark, 49; and dark chaos, 92; and description of, 92; and
  desire, 60; and without desire, 60; and discipline, 49; as effortless,
  86; as elusive, 86; as no end, 76; everywhere, 86, 104, 105; explaining, 101; and faith, 2; finding of, 6; and following, 101; and following the wisdom of, 107; when not followed, 82; and following to
  become one with the world, 89; when the foolish hear of, 6; and
  force, 91; and the use of force, 99; cannot be found, 6, 26; and governing a country, 31; and greatness, 104; and finding, 33; and finding the, 76; as formless, 86; as great, 42; and the Great Mother, 19,
  20, 60; cannot be heard, 76; as hidden, 54/18; is impartial, 56; and
  newborn infants, 24; as intangible, 86; and integrity, 19; does not

interfere, 19; and justice, 2; and kindness, 2; cannot be known, 9, 107; and laughter, 6; and law, 2; and the living valley, 97; not following as source of misfortune, 20; and this very moment, 76; as mysterious, 86; as mystery, 60, 92; as a mystery within a mystery, 86; cannot be named, 6, 107; as nameless, 60, 86; and naming the, 76; as natural, 86; and natural order, 107; like a vast net, 49; as nourishing, 104; as nourishment, 105; and oneness, 9, 60; and easy order, 101; as ordinary, 86, 104, 105; and the ordinary, 63; when the ordinary hear of, 6; path of is easy to follow, 21; and a place for everything, 33; and power, 86; as one of four great powers, 92; practiced unknowingly, 71; and primal virtue, 2; as profound, 49; and reforming, 33; is revealed, 36; and natural rhythms, 101; and ritual, 2; and a river, 101; and the sea, 101; and seeking, 33; cannot be seen, 76; as a shapeless shape, 76; as silent, 49; as simple, 101; and softening, 80; and spontaneity, 92; as subtle, 76; and the thief, 33; and each thing, 19; and thinking, 76; cannot be thought, 6, 76; as an eternal thread; 76; and trust, 2, 36; trusting, 86; understanding of, 6, 101; as unknowable, 60, 76, 86; as an inner urge, 86; use by everyone, 33; using, 86; and the valley stream, 101; value of, 33; without value it is beyond value, 26; like an empty vessel, 65; and virtue, 86; and greatest virtue, 44; and warhorses, 14; like water, 69; like deep water, 65; the way of, 15; as a wholeness, 76; and wisdom, 92; and simple wisdom, 33; when the wise hear of, 6; and wonder, 60; and the world, 20,91; and the world remains whole, 33; as wordless, 49; and words, 86

Tasks: completed and forgotten, 61

Tasting: overcome by rich flavors, 73

Teaches: without teaching, 61

Teaching: the best confuses, 13; and oneness, 95; and the sage, 11

Teachings: the ancient, 9; easy to follow, 46; no one follows the, 46; as guides, 83; rejection of, 26

Thief: and the Tao, 33

Thieves: and ingenuity, 83; and profit, 83; and valuables, 63

Thing, each: complies with the Tao, 19; shaped by itself, 19

Things: are nourished, 6; are fulfilled, 6; distracted by precious, 73; and natural rhythms of all, 101; the eternal rhythms of all, 80

Think: deeply, 69

Thinking: and names, 101; and parts, 101; and the divided wholeness, 101

Thoughts: when finally still, 71; and the Tao, 76; will never understand, 66

Thoughtlessness: and the sage receiving the world, 17

Thread: the Tao as an eternal, 76

Threat: and the path of life, 18

Threeness: and everything, 9; and twoness, 9

Timing: crucial in all situations, 69

Tranquillity: the clever as the thieves of, 38; honored, 100

Treasure: and serenity, 103; and softening, 80; and wisdom, 80

Treasures, three: compassion, 42; humility, 42; simplicity, 42

Trouble: and cleverness, 38; and making demands, 56; and dividing
     wholeness, 101; and force, 48; and guilt, 56; and knowing when to
     stop, 101; and prophets, 2; and resentment, 56; and seers, 2

Trust: and bragging, 88; and ceremony, 2; and the natural course of
     things, 35; and inner direction, 35; of the dishonest, 17; and being
     empowered, 91; of the honest, 17; and leaders, 81; and ritual, 2; and
     the way of the world, 91

Trusting: and the Way, 36

Twoness: and oneness, 9; and threeness, 9

Ugliness: created by beauty, 61

Understanding: and arguing, 41; as confusion, 4; as humility, 4; and
     knowing others, 103; and pride, 88; guided by simplicity, 63; the
     Tao, 101; and wisdom, 103

Undisciplined, the: are not favored, 49

Universe: as a bellows, 66; and emptiness, 66; does not make exceptions,
     66; and impartiality, 66

Unknown, the: guiding the sage, 2

Unworthy: the sage's feelings of being, 9

Unyielding, the: will fall, 52

Urge: that is confusing, 84; that is different, 84; from the Great Mother,
     84; that is lonely, 84

Valley: as female, 67; as mystery, 67; and nourishment, 4; and oneness, 4

Valley, living: see Living valley

Valley stream: flowing peacefully to the sea, 101; like following the Tao,
     101; joining the river, 101

Winners: in war, 45

Winter: keep moving in the cold of, 13

Wisdom: beginning of, 38; and all changing as unchanging, 80; of the
child, 71; and cleverness, 38; and entering a greater, 98; forget, 83;
the Great Mother's, 30; inherent, 95; and inner balance, 98; and
oneness, 4; of oneness, 95; and opportunity, 30; and the opposites of
the world, 98; and the sage, 98; and self, 103; of simplicity, 38; and
the Tao, 92, 107; and following the Tao, 21; of things, 46; and tranquillity, 80; and understanding, 103; and wonder, 4

Wise, the: have nothing to defend, 41; know they do not know, 47; when
they hear of the Tao, 6

Wonder: and one, 4; and oneness, 60; and the Tao, 60; and wisdom, 4

Words: the best leave nothing unsaid, 95; and description of the Tao, 92;
will never explain, 66; forgetting of, 26; these follow a principle, 46;
the most profound are simple, 41; and the Tao, 86; easy to understand, 46; no one understands the, 46

Work: and the sage, 11

World, the: and becoming one with, 89; bounty of by claiming nothing,
89; how to change, 22; and controlling it, 98; favors inner discipline,
35; doing itself, 16; entrusted with, 74; be in but do not possess, 71;
the force of, 91; and the Great Mother, 97; and improving it, 98;
known by what is, 8; living harmoniously in, 16; knowing the, 92;
and losing it, 98; moves in its own way, 8; the nature of, 97; nourish
but do not control, 71; and oneness with, 91; and opposites, 98; and
order, 46; and possessing it, 98; received as it is, 17; received
thoughtlessly, 17; and resistance of, 89; and ruining it, 98; sage does
not struggle with, 89; still thoughts and the way of, 71; straightened
by leaving crooked, 29; struggling with, 89; and the Tao, 91, 92;
trusting the way of, 91; and virtue, 22; the ways of, 98; whole
because of the Tao, 33; sage follows by yielding, 8; the way of, 15;
and the way of nature, 92; workings of as one of the four great
powers, 92; yielding and the way of, 89

Wrong: and right, 29

Yielding: the sage follows by, 8; and the ancient sages, 78; and fulfillment, 41; overcomes unyielding, 55; and overcoming, 52, 89; and
the way of the world, 89

ABOUT THE AUTHOR
RAY GRIGG

Ray Grigg has been a student and teacher of eastern philosophy for more than thirty years. Zen and Taoism in particular have been guiding forces in his life of teaching, traveling, and creative expression. He has traveled to more than forty countries, sailed in the Caribbean and the Pacific and is the author of numerous books on Taoism and Zen. He lives with his wife in a house they built on ten forested acres of Quadra Island, British Columbia, and devotes his time to writing, teaching workshops, and reading.

"Life is an art, not a science," he says. "It is an aesthetic experience that requires the wholeness in each of us to find and follow the beauty of every moment. A full and balanced life moves in harmony with the dynamics of the immediate present."

ABOUT THE ILLUSTRATOR
WILLIAM GAETZ

A consuming interest in art, philosophy, and religious studies has occupied the life of William Gaetz. An accomplished vocalist and classical pianist, he is also a teacher of Zen and Metaphysics. After years of expressing his creativity through photography, he embarked on the path of Chinese brush painting under the tutelage of Master Professor Peng Kung Yi. This is the medium that he feels best fulfills his spiritual needs and comes closest to expressing the inexpressible. *The New Lao Tzu* is the fourth book by Ray Grigg that William Gaetz has illustrated. In these pieces, Mr. Gaetz has used a special "thrown ink" style that is both old and new, one that honors the ancient tradition of China, but is also contemporary and innovative.

William Gaetz presently lives in Victoria, British Columbia and contines to paint under the Chinese name of Koy Sai. His work is shown in Victoria galleries, and hangs in homes and businesses throughout Canada and the United States.